Lisa Whelchel

Speaking
mom-ese

Lisa Whelchel

Speaking mom-ese

Moments of Peace
& Inspiration
in the **Mother Tongue**
from one mom's heart to yours

THOMAS NELSON
Since 1798

NASHVILLE   DALLAS   MEXICO CITY   RIO DE JANEIRO   BEIJING

Published in Nashville, Tennessee, by Thomas Nelson. Thomas Nelson is a trademark of Thomas Nelson, Inc.

Thomas Nelson, Inc. books may be purchased in bulk for educational, business, fund-raising, or sales promotional use. For information, please e-mail SpecialMarkets@ThomasNelson.com.

Scripture references are from the following sources: The Holy Bible, New Living Translation (NLT), © 1996. Used by permission of Tyndale House Publishers, Inc., Wheaton, Illinois 60189. NEW AMERICAN STANDARD BIBLE ® (NASB), © 1960, 1962, 1963, 1968, 1971, 1972, 1973, 1975, 1977, 1995 by The Lockman Foundation. Used by permission. The Message (MSG), © 1993. Used by permission of NavPress Publishing Group. The Holy Bible, New International Version (NIV). © 1973, 1978, 1983, International Bible Society. Used by permission of Zondervan Bible Publishers. The Holy Bible, New Century Version (NCV), © 1987, 1988, 1991 by Word Publishing, Dallas, Texas 75234. Used by permission. The New International Reader's Version® (NIRV®). © 1996, 1998 International Bible Society. All rights reserved throughout the world. Used by permission of International Bible Society.

[1]My Utmost for His Highest: Selections for the Year. The Golden Book of Oswald Chambers. New York: Dodd, Mead & Co., 1944, p.211.

Cover Design: Brand Navigation, www.brandnavigation.com
Interior Design: Susan Browne Design/Nashville, TN

ISBN 10: 1-59145-345-3 (hc)
ISBN 13: 978-1-59145-345-1 (hc)
ISBN 10: 0-7852-8930-5 (tp)
ISBN 13: 978- 0-7852-8930-2 (tp)

Printed in the United States of America
07 08 09 10 11 RRD 6 5 4 3 2 1

This book, like my original journal entries,
is written to and for my "cyber friends."
I can't wait to live next door to
each one of you in heaven.

The heartfelt counsel of a friend is
as sweet as perfume and incense.

—*Proverbs 27:9 NLT*

table of contents

thank you, thank you, thank you
(or "Acknowledgements")

Steve, Tucker, Haven, and Clancy—Thank you for the sacrifices you make so that I may serve other families.

Laura Minchew and Integrity Publishing—Thank you for your patience as I attempt to balance being a mother with writing for mothers.

Criswell Freeman—Thank you for your exhaustive help and words of encouragement. I am honored to work with you.

Betsy Holt—Thank you, once again, for adding your magical touch!

Glenda Murray—Thank you for believing that someone else would want to read this stuff.

Mary Hollingsworth—Thank you for mining the nuggets and calling them gold.

Ron Smith—Thank you for being my defender and protector.

Mike Goldberg and LionZone Web Design—Thank you for coming in many a weekend so I could serve a fresh "Coffee Talk" on Monday mornings.

Al and Tracie Denson—Thank you for allowing me to hole away at your beautiful ranch to write. You are truly "hysterical" givers.

Dyke and Raynayle Ferrell—Thank you for the use of your adorable cabin to pray and edit.

hello, my name is lisa
(or "The Introduction")

I've heard a lot of great teaching in my life. I've read a bunch
of good books. I've listened to some amazing pastors. But without a doubt, the words that have had the greatest impact on my
life occurred during conversations at the kitchen table, talking
to moms just like you. Maybe it's because I know you're strug-
gling with the same challenges I'm facing. Perhaps it's because
your wisdom has been mined in the trenches of experience, not
just read about in a book. Whatever the reason, I've decided that
moms really do know best.

There's definitely some kind of sister synergy or mommy
momentum that happens when moms get together to compare
notes. We speak each other's language. We can finish each other's
sentences. We've been there, _____ _____. (See? I bet you
filled in those blanks with "wiped that.") Moms understand each
other. Sometimes I think English is our second language and our
mother tongue is Mom–ese.

Here's a little vocational vocabulary test I put together for fun. Don't worry—if you're reading this book then I'm sure you'll pass it.

Define the following terms:

a. Binky

b. Pull-Ups

c. Nurse

d. Let down

e. Braxton-Hicks

f. Dora

g. Boo-boo

h. PB&J

i. Pampers

j. Wooden spoon

k. Permit

l. Cradle cap

m. Changing pad

n. Aspirator

o. Curfew

p. *Goodnight Moon*

q. The pink stuff

r. Breast pump

If you answered:

a. Disney character

b. Pectoral exercises

c. R.N.

d. Disappoint

e. Law firm

f. Italian entrance

g. Two ghosts

h. Rap artist

i. Indulges

j. Stirring utensil

k. Allow

l. Crib lid

m. Apartment

n. Dreamer

o. Time boundary

p. When your spouse turns over in bed

q. You have no idea

r. You don't dare answer

...then I'm not sure you'll want to read this book. You just won't get it. On the other hand, if you answered:

a. Plug

b. Big girl panties

c. Got milk?

d. Filling up "the bottle"

e. Labor rehearsal

f. Spanish explorer

g. Excuse for an Elmo Band-Aid

h. Lunch staple (without the crust)

i. Budget buster

j. When time-outs don't work

k. A "license to drive" Mom to her knees

l. Dandruff without the hair

m. Thing you use on your mother-in-law's couch

n. Nose sucker

o. The only time Mom stays up later than her teens

p. Book you could read in your sleep (and have)

q. Amoxicillin

r. Dairy farm

...then keep reading, 'cause you're going to love this book! In fact, you'll wonder if you're reading your own autobiography. How do I know that? Because mothers know these things. We have eyes in the back of our heads, remember? And I can already see you laughing and crying (sometimes at the same time) as you recognize yourself inside the pages of this book.

These devotions are lifted directly from my life as a mom. They are snippets of my experiences—both the good and the not so good—as I've parented my kids from the demanding toddler years to the hormonal teenage years. To make this book feel more like a journal, I've included a few blank lines after each devotion to give you the opportunity to "Speak Mom-ese" and then end with a two-way conversation between you and God. My hope is that these brief stories, thoughts, and prayers, which have been written especially for busy moms like you, will help you find support, encouragement, and even a few moments of rest.

I know how difficult it can be to find time to reflect and pray. When my kids were tiny, I had virtually no time to pour out my heart in my journal. Over the years, I have collected approximately fifteen journals, all with about a dozen entries in them that end somewhere around the middle of February. My husband, Steve, eventually bought a computer journal for me, which helped quite a bit. But the real breakthrough came when I began posting my journal entries on my website. Soon, my cyber friends began joining me for "Coffee Talk," and now rarely a week goes by that I don't blog my joys and frustrations, hopes and fears. I can attest that the simple act of writing down my thoughts and swapping stories and prayer requests with my Internet pals has been a tremendous blessing. (And believe me, I need all the support I can get now that my kids are teenagers!)

Having children will put you on life's most exhilarating—and exhausting—roller coaster ride. There are times I feel like I'm just a little girl, playing house. (So, you wanna come over and play?) Then at other times, I feel like I'm becoming my mother and my children are payback for the stress I put her through! (On second thought, why don't you come over and we'll *pray*?) But most often, I'm extremely thankful for the privilege of being a mommy, and I'm eternally grateful for my heavenly Father, who helps guide me along the way.

I think we're going to be great friends, don't you?

the proverbs 31 woman

. . . .

**"There are many virtuous and capable women in
the world, but you surpass them all!"**

Proverbs 31:29 NLT

I don't know about you, but the superwoman featured in
Proverbs 31 intimidates me! When I'm reading that passage,
I'm tempted to jump ahead to the book of Ecclesiastes, where
the theme "everything is vanity" is considerably closer to where
I live. One day out of frustration, I asked the Lord why He would
put such a seemingly unattainable example of motherhood in
the Bible. *That "perfect" woman*, I vented to Him, *makes the rest
of us feel like failures in comparison!*

When God answered, He spoke right to my heart. *Because
that is how I see her—as flawless, but that is how I see you, too,*
He told me gently. *I see all of the good things you've ever done or*

will do. Remember, all your sins are covered by My Son's blood. They are gone.

I suddenly understood that I should read Proverbs 31 from my heavenly Father's perspective—that of a proud and loving parent. It makes sense, doesn't it? For example, if my mother were to write a paragraph describing me, she would probably say, "My daughter, Lisa, is an amazing woman. She graduated from high school as valedictorian. She's a Grammy-nominated singer, a creative mother, an actress on a hit television series, and a loving wife. She's made millions of dollars! She's a ballet, tap, and jazz dancer; a glider pilot; a talented musician; and a great cook. She teaches multiple grades; keeps a beautiful home; her nails always look gorgeous; she sews her children's clothes; she keeps a record of their lives in scrapbooks; she's up before dawn having her devotions; she wears designer clothes; *and* she's a record-setting race car driver."

Now, the description above is true, but it leaves out several pieces of significant information. For starters, I've accomplished those things over the course of forty years; I don't do them all now. That account also gives just half the story. It leaves out many of my secrets—embarrassing secrets that only my mom knows.

Here's my life story as *I* see it:

"Lisa is an amazing woman (some of the time). She gradu-ated from high school as valedictorian (there were three students in her graduating class). She's a Grammy-nominated singer (who recorded each line of the song multiple times so that the engineer could manage to piece together an entire song that was on pitch), a creative mother (if you don't count the yelling), an actress on a hit television series (who almost got fired for getting too fat), and a loving wife (except for years two through seven). She's made millions of dollars (and lost it all). She's a ballet, tap, and jazz dancer (the worst in her class); a glider pilot (who hasn't flown since she got her license); a talented musician (who can play two songs on the guitar); and a great cook (if you count her two standard "company" meals). She teaches multiple grades at the same time (with only one child in each class), keeps a beautiful home (with the help of a once-a-week housekeeper), her nails always look gorgeous (they're fake), she sews her children's clothes (actually, the sewing machine hasn't been touched in years), keeps a record of their lives in scrapbooks (she's three years behind), she's up before dawn having her devotions (well, *most* days of the week), she wears designer clothes (on the set, that a wardrobe person picks out), and she's a record-setting race car driver (at the Malibu Grand Prix go-cart track)."

Now, both of the perspectives above are true, but one of them is told through the eyes of a loving parent. I believe that even more than our parents would, our heavenly Father would write a glowing description of us, too. As He reminded me, He sees the good in us. When we put our faith in Him, He chooses not to remember our mistakes and instead focuses on our successes. So, from God's perspective, maybe the "Proverbs 31 woman" isn't so unattainable after all.

Write at least a dozen nice things about yourself from your heavenly Father's perspective. _____

Speaking
m o m - e s e

_____

_____

_____

_____

_____

_____

_____

_____

_____

_____

_____

_____

_____

Prayer

Lord, thank You for being such a loving parent. I am so grateful that You see the good in me, even when I mess up or fall short of where I think I should be. Help me not to compare myself to other moms and to focus instead on Your love and Your desires for my life.

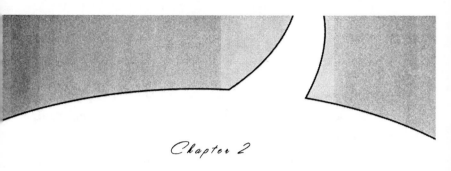

i feel your pain

. . . .

Blessed be the God and Father of our Lord Jesus Christ, the Father of mercies and God of all comfort, who comforts us in all our tribulation, that we may be able to comfort those who are in any trouble, with the comfort with which we ourselves are comforted by God.

2 Corinthians 1:3–4 NKJV

I have never known stress like I did when I was raising three toddlers. At least a half dozen times a day, my "angels" would make me want to scream at the top of my lungs and cry. They just wouldn't do what I wanted them to do. They argued and were unkind to each other. They constantly whined, "Hold me. Hold me." They threw fits. Sometimes they even battled with me for hours—simply over cleaning their rooms.

Of course, this makes them sound horrible, and they're not! In general, Tucker, Haven, and Clancy are great kids. It's just that they weren't born well-behaved. No child is. So, I often had to wage a war to get them to submit to me and to the high calling of Jesus Christ.

There were times I felt I was spanking them all day long and it wasn't doing any good. On those days, I couldn't spank them any more; I couldn't encourage and praise them any more. I knew I could always pray more, but even prayer seemed ineffective. It felt like nothing would reduce the stress except for time. Specifically, twenty years of time.

With all that chaos, trying to fit in anything to do for myself was really frustrating. My goals for each day were simple: I wanted to exercise, journal, sew a bit, take a bath, make the bed, and keep the kitchen clean. I didn't usually attain all those goals, but I did learn to adjust my expectations. I wrote in my journal once a week or so. Exercised at least every other day. Sewed once a season. Made the bed before Steve got home. Bathed if I could. And cleaned the high chair if things started growing on it.

If I was able to accomplish these things; if the kids were all healthy and taking their naps or playing quietly in their rooms, then life suddenly made sense. But I don't think I ever experienced more than two of those days, let alone two hours at a stretch. I simply did the best I could, as I'm sure you do, too.

I share all this with you because I know what it's like to be in the trenches. I've been a mom long enough to know that sometimes, the most encouraging words you can hear are the ones that remind you that you are not alone.

Whatever you're experiencing, you can bet I've been there, too. I feel your pain!

Just hang in there—some things *will* get easier.

· ·

Speaking
m o m - e s e

Write down your frustrations as a mom. Believe it or not, it is good to have a record of the negative as well as the positive. _____

_____

_____

_____

_____

_____

_____

_____

_____

_____

_____

_____

_____

_____

Prayer
Thank You, Lord, for walking with me through every season.
When the winds of life begin to blow, help me to hang on tight and weather
the storms. Allow me to comfort others who are going through similar
rough times.

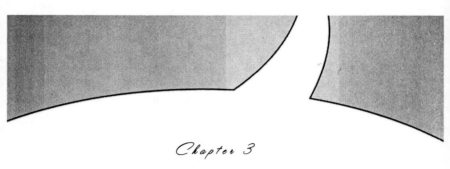

Chapter 3

thank God for family

. . . .

So we, who are many, are one body in Christ, and individually members one of another.

Romans 12:5 NASB

It was quite a day. All three kids were sick. My mom, normally so helpful, was busy with her own things, and Steve had left town the day before. Clancy had a fever of 104.5 degrees, Haven's was just under 102, and Tucker's hovered around 101. I was exhausted after a night of off-and-on sleep and was aching for a nap. Unfortunately, the kids were never down all at one time.

I spent 80 percent of the day sitting in the La-Z-Boy with a very sick child on each knee, watching videos. The rest of the time, I gave tepid baths to bring fevers down and doled out Triaminic and the "pink stuff." Clancy was particularly miserable. She would not let me put her down for one minute. Haven insisted

I sit with her as she picked out something like one hundred videos for her viewing pleasure. And Tucker...well, Tucker had gone over the edge—about everything. All self-control, obedience, and cheerfulness had flown out the window.

Yet, what a difference the body of Christ makes! That afternoon, a friend from church, Naomi, called to get Steve's fax number in Virginia. When she asked me how things were going, I told her—in excruciating detail. Five minutes after I hung up the phone, my friend Darrylyn called and said she had just talked to Naomi. Was there anything she could do to help? I didn't want to admit that I needed anything, but no amount of pride could disguise my weary voice.

Darrylyn ended up coming over late that afternoon to help bathe the kids, get them to bed, and straighten up around the house. The kids and I both loved the company and the help. Later I found out that Pastor Scott had asked the church to pray for us, too. When I heard that, I realized it wasn't just the cool bath and fresh company Darrylyn provided that helped, but also the prayers of the saints.

The Lord had a brilliant plan when He devised the body of Christ, the family of God. Your biological family may not live close enough to help you through those "sick-and-tired" days, but if you are part of a local body of believers, then you have spiritual brothers and sisters, moms and dads all around you. I've heard many well-meaning people say that you don't have to go to church to be a Christian. That may be true, but why would anyone want to go through life without a family of believers?

We have a plaque at home that reads "Families Are Forever." When I purchased it, I was thinking about my immediate blood relatives. I've since realized however, that my church family is also forever—they'll be with me for eternity!

. . . .

Speaking mom-ese

If you don't know very many people at your church, jot down a few ideas for becoming more involved so you can develop some relationships. Or write down the names of people in your church who could use a touch of encouragement or practical help from a member of the family of God. _____

_____

_____

_____

_____

_____

_____

_____

_____

Prayer

Thank You, Father, for the reminder that You "setteth the solitary in families" (see Psalm 68:6). We, as Christians, need each other, and You know that. Help me not to be too prideful or embarrassed to ask for help. Then, in turn, encourage me to reach out to help others.

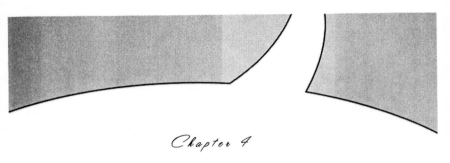

Chapter 4

my career as a mother

. . . .

"For I know the plans I have for you," declares the Lord, "plans to prosper you and not to harm you, plans to give you hope and a future."

Jeremiah 29:11 NIV

I was at a Hearts At Home conference in Michigan. Founded by speaker and author Jill Savage, the seminars are designed to provide support and encouragement to stay-at-home moms. On the way home from the conference, I read Jill's book *Professionalizing Motherhood*. What a great concept! In her book, she observes that many women feel like they have left more "respectable" professions to become stay-at-home moms. But Jill reminds women that when we decide to stay home with our kids, we simply take all of the gifts, talents, intelligence, creativity, work ethic, and passion—things we had previously brought to the workforce—and apply those skills to the profession of motherhood.

I had never thought of motherhood that way, and the idea was freeing. Her perspective also came at a perfect time since I was trying to overhaul the way I balanced family and ministry. Jill's words released me to begin applying some of the things I had learned in the business world to my job as a mom.

I followed her advice and decided to set some goals. I began by writing out objectives for the remainder of the year, goals for the following year, and finally, goals I wanted to accomplish before my children left home. The list included things I want to teach my children, such as establishing a personal devotional time with Jesus, pursuing God to find their calling in life, and living out the spiritual and moral values they have been taught. Some of my other objectives included goals for the entire family, like reading more books aloud together, playing more games together, and cooking together. Once I began to write these things down, I realized I had definite goals for my home, my marriage, and my ministry.

I've heard many stay-at-home mothers describe themselves this way: "I'm just a mom." That's like saying, "I'm just an astronaut," or "I'm just a Supreme Court Justice." Motherhood is not just any old job. It's undeniably one of the most important jobs in God's creation!

Regardless of whether you're a stay-at-home mom or a mom that works outside the home, you understand the critical importance of raising your children with love, with discipline, and with God. You know that your overriding purpose is to care for your family and to teach them the ways of the Lord. So, why not take the time to write down your goals? It won't take long, paper is cheap, and you just might learn something about yourself or your loved ones.

One thing I've realized about setting goals is that they can remain lofty dreams if I don't also make definite plans and appropriate changes to implement them. To reach my goals, I designated Tuesday mornings as family read-aloud time and Thursday afternoons as game day. Then, I put these "appointments" on my calendar. To be honest, there are still many times I edge out these important time slots and choose the "tyranny of the urgent" over investing in my goals for the future. But that's part of life. You can't always meet every milestone. Don't beat yourself up over the goals you don't attain, and don't expect perfection from yourself or your family. Remember this: no family is perfect, not even yours—and that's perfectly okay.

· ·

Speaking
mom-ese

Write down the goals you have for
yourself and your family. Now identify the changes or plans you need
to implement to make your goals a
reality. _____

_____

_____
_____
_____
_____
_____
_____
_____
_____
_____
_____
_____
_____
_____
_____
_____
_____
_____

Prayer
Lord, give me Your vision for my family. Let me see where You are working
and where You're headed. Allow me to set goals that are in line with the
plans You have for our future. Empower me to follow through on my good
intentions. Thank You for giving me the best job ever—being a mother!

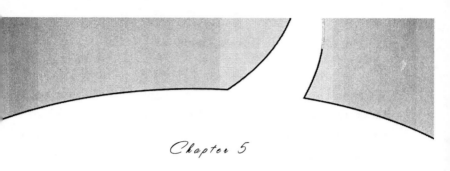

a tongue of fire

· ·

**So also the tongue is a small part of the body, and
yet it boasts of great things. See how great a forest
is set aflame by such a small fire!**

James 3:5 NASB

What a week! It all started when the *Washington Post*
printed an article about "hot saucing" as a form of correction,
quoting me and my book *Creative Correction* extensively. A few
days later, I was asked to be on *Fox News* and then *Good Morning America*. The night before I appeared on *GMA*, the show
conducted an informal website poll, to which, over three hundred
thousand people responded. According to the poll, 65 percent felt
that using hot sauce was an unacceptable form of discipline.
Then, the next morning, when I was being interviewed, the show
brought in a doctor who said the correction was "barbaric" and
likened it to "chemical warfare."

Now, I'm all for talking and reasoning with children, but I think any parent would agree that it is not always effective to use words alone as a method of correction. There are times when concrete consequences can teach abstract concepts, whereas a million wise words or time-outs won't do a thing.

I'm not referring to silly, "kids will be kids" kinds of issues, like tracking mud in the living room and running through the house. I'm talking about the fact that there are some lessons in life that are not worth leaving up to chance or to my children to figure out on their own. (Things like lying, stealing, and learning respect for authority come to mind.) Training them for life is my responsibility—and privilege. And, I don't think it's a stretch to believe that if I can teach my children about the gravity of lying with the sting of a drop of hot sauce, then, conceivably, I could spare them the exponential pain of divorce, because trustworthiness is critical in marriage. I would rather cause my children a small amount of pain from my hand of love if it spares them a much greater amount of pain later in life. In fact, the Bible says, "No discipline is enjoyable while it is happening—it is painful! But afterward there will be a quiet harvest of right living for those who are trained in this way" (Hebrews 12:11 NLT).

Is it any wonder that today's generation has very little respect for authority? Moms and dads are afraid to parent with firmness and are praised for being friends with their children. I'm friends with my kids, too—in fact, we are very close—but first and foremost, I will always be their parent. If need be, friendship can come later. I don't want to visit my "friend" in jail while a police officer teaches my child about respect for authority.

I liked Tucker's take on the whole controversy best. On the way to an interview on *Fox News*, he offered to vouch for the fact that I'm not really a whacked-out child star turned child abuser. "Therths nothing wrong with Tabathco thauths," Tucker said with his "numb tongue." "I can't tasthe anything, but I don't tell lieths anymore!"

. . . .

What is your opinion about "tough love"? If spanking or using Tabasco sauce are not forms of correction you are comfortable with, then write down a few methods of discipline you feel would be effective when tough times call for tough measures.

Speaking mom-ese

_____
_____
_____
_____
_____
_____
_____
_____
_____
_____
_____
_____
_____
_____
_____
_____
_____

Prayer

Lord, help me to remember that correction and love are not mutually exclusive. Give me the wisdom to know when a gentle word of encouragement or even a stern reprimand is best, and the courage to use effective discipline when words alone aren't enough.

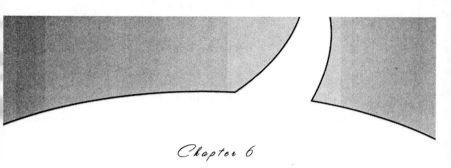

Chapter 6

clean me up, Lord

. . . .

**If we confess our sins, he is faithful and just
and will forgive us our sins and purify us from
all unrighteousness.**

1 John 1:9 NIV

Haven was having trouble getting along with Clancy. It was mostly Haven's fault, but she kept trying to point the finger at her little sister. When I pressed her about it, Haven admitted that she really didn't want to do what it would take to get along with Clancy because it was "too hard," and she didn't think she could do it.

To help her see the problem with her thinking, I told her the following story:

"Haven, imagine that you are getting up from the breakfast table when you knock over the cereal box and scatter corn flakes all over the floor," I began. "Immediately, you blame Clancy for not closing the box top after using it. While Clancy has been a little careless, you are the one who knocked over the cereal box, so it is your responsibility to clean it up. If you don't clean up your mess, before long, the kitchen will be covered in cereal crumbs and your breakfast will be tracked throughout the house. If you simply sweep the cereal under the throw rug in front of the sink, water might spill onto the floor and mix with the cereal, eventually forming a green and black breakfast stew. In time, the kitchen will begin to stink—something that inevitably happens when we try to hide our problems instead of dealing with them."

Of course, Haven had admitted her role in the problem (though not without my pressing her!). So, to drive the point home further, I then asked her to picture a slightly different scenario:

"Now imagine, that after knocking over the cereal box, you acknowledge you made a mistake and ask for help. Soon, a man shows up to help you. Still, you whine, saying, 'But I don't have what it takes to clean it up.'

"'That's okay,' the man replies. 'I have the tools. You hold this dustpan, and I'll sweep it up and take it away.'

"But instead of holding the dustpan, you leave the room to let the man do all the work. When you return, you are surprised to find the pile of corn flake crumbs still there, swept neatly into the middle of the floor.

"You confront the man, saying, 'Hey, you promised you would clean it up for me.'

"'I did clean things up,' the man answers, 'but you needed to do your part if you *really* wanted the mess to go away.'"

The moral of the story, as I explained to Haven, is this: it's okay to admit that we don't want to face our sins or that we don't think we can deal with them. We just have to admit to God (and our parents!) that we have sinned and ask Him to help us clean up our lives. When we do, He brings the tools and even takes care of our mess. But we have to ask, and we have to help—even if all we do is remain still and hold on while He does the work.

. . . .

Speaking
mom-ese

Write down at least one area of your life
that you'd like to change. You may
even need to confess that you've
tried changing and have failed, or
that you don't really feel like trying
but know that you need to. Just be
completely honest with God; He can
handle it. Then, confess that you need His help to change
and humbly ask for His power to do so._____

_____
_____
_____
_____
_____
_____
_____
_____
_____
_____
_____
_____
_____
_____
_____

Prayer

*Lord, I know I've blown it in this area time and time again. Once more, I
come to You and ask You to forgive me. Thank You for having fresh mercy on
me every day. I really do want to change. And I really do need Your help. So,
here I am asking. Thank You in advance for answering my prayer.*

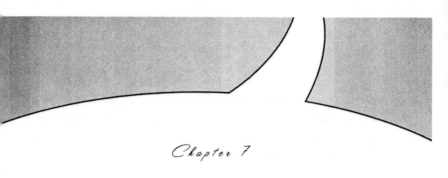

double or nothing

· ·

**Give, and it will be given to you. A good measure,
pressed down, shaken together and running over,
will be poured into your lap. For with the measure
you use, it will be measured to you.**

Luke 6:38 NIV

$\mathcal{S}$teve, the children, and I had just enjoyed a wonderful evening with my brother and his family. We had eaten at a Mexican restaurant, and both, the food and the company, had been great. The most memorable part of the evening however was yet to come.

On the drive back home, Tucker pulled out—get ready for this—not one, but two loose teeth! (So if all you want for Christmas is your two front teeth, I can cut you a deal, at least on two back teeth.) Tucker immediately launched into negotiations, declaring that because he had pulled two teeth at once, he deserved a double reward from me (oops, I mean the tooth fairy!). I tried to convince Tucker that I had not yet been able to sell any of his old teeth, so that meant his used pearly whites, when removed from his mouth, were worth zippo. And, of course, two times zip equals zero. Still, Tucker wasn't buying it.

That night after Tucker had fallen soundly asleep, I slipped into my tights and wings to perform my fairy duties. When I pulled the Ziploc bag holding his two teeth from under his pillow, there was a sticky note attached that read "Mom—More Money!" Tucker's financial negotiations, it seems, were ongoing even while he slept.

As grownups, we may be too big to believe in the tooth fairy, but we still act like children occasionally, especially when it comes to money. We always want more. Martin Luther even struggled with greed, admitting, "Many things I have tried to grasp and have lost. That which I have placed in God's hands I still have."

That quote reminds me of a "Toolbox" suggestion in my book *Creative Correction*. As an object lesson to teach children that we can never out-give God, I instruct moms to give their child a quarter and have him close his hand and hold the coin very tightly to keep it from slipping through his fingers. Then, I tell moms to take a jar of change and empty it over the child's clenched fist. How much money does he have now? Still a quarter!

Next, I instruct moms to ask their child to hold the coin in his hand, but this time to tell him to keep his palm open while a jar of change is poured over it. Now how much money does he have? A lot more than a measly quarter!

God loves to give good gifts to His children. The irony is that we must live open-handedly if we are to experience His abundance. If we're always thinking about what we can get, how to keep it, and how to acquire even more, we limit God's ability to bless us more lavishly than we could ever imagine.

· ·

Speaking
m o m - e s e

What has God given to you that you could use to bless others? What items could you give away? What items could you let others borrow? Make a list of things you own that could make a difference in someone else's life if you held them a little more loosely.

_____

_____

_____

_____

_____

_____

_____

_____

_____

_____

_____

_____

_____

_____

_____

_____

Prayer

God, You have blessed me with so much. Please forgive me when I negotiate for even more. Help me to be grateful for, and open-handed with, the undeserved gifts You give me. Change my heart to be more unselfish like Yours. Help me to learn to love giving even more than receiving.

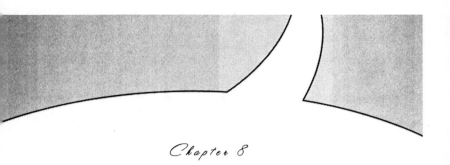

"little ones" are a big deal to God

. . . .

Whatever you do, work at it with all your heart, as working for the Lord, not for men.

Colossians 3:23 NIV

As I listened to Matthew Barnett speak, I was moved by his work at the Dream Center in downtown Los Angeles. The place bills itself as "The Church That Never Sleeps" because its doors are always open—seven days a week, twenty-four hours a day.

There, Matthew and his staff minister physically, emotionally, and spiritually to the homeless, AIDS victims, gang members, moms on welfare, and abandoned kids.

I must admit that the longer he spoke, the more insignificant I began to feel. *After all,* I told myself, *I've been called to minister to moms. But Matthew has been called to do "tougher" work in the inner city.* The comparison made my ministry look like a cakewalk.

At the end of his message, Matthew asked if we would like for God to "break our hearts with love for others." His words touched me deeply, and the moment the congregation was able to come forward, I jumped to my feet and made my way to the front of the church. I knelt down, buried my face in the carpet, and cried until my tears soaked the floor. When I did this, the Lord chastised me gently, telling me that He doesn't compare me to His other children and neither should I.

He reminded me, *your mission field is young children, and the best way for you to reach them is by ministering to their mothers. It isn't as dramatic as preaching to prostitutes and drug dealers on the streets of Los Angeles, but your desire to help moms to know Me and experience My joy in the practical, everyday matters of life isn't any less important.*

Then God drove His point closer to home. As I continued to cry, I felt a tiny tap on my shoulder. It was my daughter Clancy, who had worked up the courage to find me at the front of the church. She, too, had been crying. When I asked her about her tears, she said, "Mommy, I don't know why I'm crying, because on the inside, I'm smiling."

I explained to her that she was in the presence of the Lord, and that because God's presence is so overwhelming, sometimes the only response that seems big enough is to cry. As I stood behind Clancy, with my arms around her, I saw her lift her little hands in the air. What a moment. What a memory. What a privilege. I walked away with fresh confidence knowing that reaching little ones and their moms is a big deal to God.

. . . .

Speaking mom-ese

Think of your family and neighborhood as your mission field. The ways you take care of your children each day are an act of ministry, but what are some other opportunities you have to serve those around you? Make a list of the things you do that may seem insignificant to you but in God's eyes are part of His calling on your life. _____

_____

_____

_____

_____

_____

_____

_____

_____

_____

_____

_____

_____

_____

_____

_____

Prayer

Father God, freshly anoint me for the mission of ministering to my children through simple acts of service, obedience, and love. Help me to seize every opportunity to be used by You. Remind me not to compare myself with others. Instead, break my heart with love for those around me so that in focusing on the "small things," I might make a big difference.

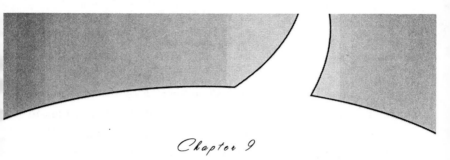

the real telephone game

· ·

**Though some tongues just love the taste of gossip,
Christians have better uses for language than that.**

Ephesians 5:4 MSG

For many years, we met three other families in Oxnard, California, for a big summer vacation. The first year, we had fourteen children under the age of six. Can you imagine what it was like when our group showed up at a restaurant? "Yes, I would like a table for twenty-two, please. I'll need twelve children's menus, two booster seats, two highchairs, and four checks."

The vacation began when everybody arrived on Sunday afternoon. Our standing joke was that, if we could survive check-in, the rest of the week would be easy. Procuring four rooms next door to each other, all facing the beach, was no mean task in the middle of the summer season. But somehow, we seemed to manage.

After we had all unpacked and gotten comfortable in our rooms, we headed down to the hotel restaurant. We learned to reserve our own special room with one humongous table. Then we played the "telephone" game while we waited for our food.

Do you remember that childhood game? One person starts the chain by whispering a phrase into the next person's ear, who in turn whispers to the person next to her, and so on until everyone has whispered something. The last person announces what she hears, and it is usually a funny variation of the original phrase.

The game is a lot of fun, but it also teaches children—and adults, too—a powerful message about gossip. Gossip is a big temptation for most of us. We humans seem to have some deep-seated desire to pass things on about other people and the not-so-nice things they do from time to time. Often, as with the game of telephone, our words get increasingly twisted (and usually more hurtful) as they are passed from person to person. When we engage in the sin of gossip, we invariably hurt other people and ourselves in the process.

Our words have great power. If they are encouraging, they can lift others up; if they are hurtful, they can hold others back. The Bible reminds us that "reckless words pierce like a sword, but the tongue of the wise brings healing" (Proverbs 12:18 NIV). In other words, if we are to be God's helpers and problem solvers, we must measure our words carefully.

God's Word makes it perfectly clear: "If you claim to be religious but don't control your tongue, you are just fooling yourself, and your religion is worthless" (James 1:26 NLT). Do yourself, your family, and your friends a big favor. Don't waste your breath with gossip. Not only is it a waste of words, it's the wrong thing to do. When you play the gossip game, everybody loses.

. . . .

Speaking
mom-ese

What are some subtle ways that you gossip? Jot them down. Now write down ways that your style of communicating can influence, both positively and negatively, how your children learn to communicate. Go back and underline the ways in which you can positively encourage your children to use their words to bring life instead of death (see Proverbs 18:21).

_____

_____

_____

_____

_____

_____

_____

_____

_____

_____

_____

_____

_____

_____

_____

Prayer

Father, forgive me for the times I have spoken about Your children behind their backs. I'm sorry for making a game out of the personal things in other people's lives. When I am confronted with gossip disguised as a prayer request, prompt me to hang up the "telephone" and pray privately.

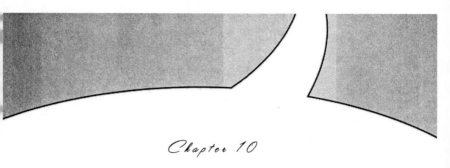

watch out for scooters!

. . . .

**And I tell you that you are Peter, and on this rock
I will build my church, and the gates of Hades will
not overcome it.**

Matthew 16:18 NIV

I was sitting in our hotel room one summer vacation, reading a book. The author was talking about Jesus' disciples, including the dynamic brothers John and James—called the "Sons of Thunder"—and Peter, who was zealous about God but famous for always getting into trouble. The author made the point that Jesus was able to take these men, who were extremely rough, raw material, and use them to build His church.

While I was reading this passage, Tucker appeared from the back door of the hotel room and flew past me, on his scooter, out the front door into the hallway. Without realizing it, I simply glanced at him and smiled. When I did, Tucker looked back and said, "I love you, Mom!" Most mothers would probably scream instead of smile if their sons rode through a hotel room on a scooter. (Of course, I probably would have, too, if I hadn't just been reading about the marvelous things that God can do with rough-and-tumble guys like Tucker.)

Not long after the scooter incident, God taught me to appreciate Haven in a similar way. My middle child was having a particularly stinky attitude. She was fighting Steve and me about everything. It was one of her "if-you-say-it's-black, I'll-say-it's-white" days. In the midst of this negativity, our family saw the movie *Seabiscuit*. The title character is a horse that initially seems impossible to train. Seabiscuit is challenging, feisty—and yet, full of incredible potential.

I saw much of Haven in that underdog-turned-champion horse. Her strong will, fierce competitiveness, passion, and individuality allows her to look life straight in the eye and say, "Bring it on. Show me what you've got. Because I've got Jesus!" Those characteristics may make her more challenging to parent at times, but they will always put her in the winner's circle.

I like to read biographies, and in my reading, I've realized that very few famous people were compliant children. Most of them were strong-willed, had ADHD, or exhibited learning disabilities that we as a culture are always trying to "cure." I'd like to think that God, who has given all of us different gifts, different opportunities, and different personalities, celebrates His children just as they are. There is no limit to what He can do with our lives if we are willing.

Are you the mom of a strong-willed child? If so, remember that Jesus chose disciples who were, by all accounts, as determined as they were faithful. If your child has a streak of stubbornness or an innate ability to find—or create—mischief, don't despair. I assure you that God has big plans for that child, and He obviously thinks you are the perfect mother for the job, or He wouldn't have given you the task.

· ·

Speaking
mom-ese

Make a list of some of the more challenging aspects of your children's
personalities. Now, think about how
God may use those very qualities,
redeemed by His Spirit, to change
the world. _____

_____

_____

_____

_____

_____

_____

_____

_____

_____

_____

_____

_____

_____

_____

_____

_____

_____

_____

Prayer

*Help me not to grow weary, Jesus, as I attempt to raise these demanding,
sometimes frustrating, often exhausting children. I know You have great
plans for their lives. Encourage me when I forget this and enable me to
build up my little ones when they, too, get discouraged.*

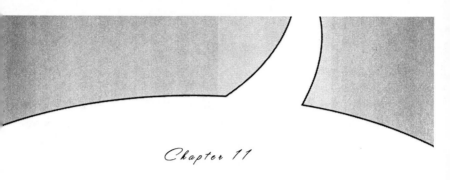

would i rather be right or righteous?

. . . .

By this we know love, because He laid down His life for us. And we also ought to lay down our lives for the brethren.

1 John 3:16 NKJV

My ability to form instant opinions and quick answers has always been a plus for me. It helps me in my parenting, my business decisions, and in my ministry. Over the years, though, God has taught me that I shouldn't always say everything I feel or think. I can wait and pray about things before I comment on them. It is not a virtue to be able to form a winning argument before the person I'm speaking with has even finished talking!

During one particular season in life, I journaled a lot about my struggle to always be right. In one entry I wrote, "The Lord is really taking me through open-heart surgery. I know it sounds strange, but I'm finally at the place where I'm willing to believe that there are no exceptions to what the Bible says. When Scripture says, 'Be slow to anger and slow to speak' [see James 1:19], it doesn't mean, 'Except for you, Lisa. I admire your quickness.'"

This desire to be right makes it challenging for me to "turn the other cheek." The Bible teaches that as Steve's wife, I am called to follow his leadership, and sometimes that entails giving up the privilege to be right. Most of the time when we're fighting, I would rather let tensions boil between us, because I feel Steve has wronged me and that it's his place to come to me, repent, and resolve the conflict. But even if Steve is acting like a real pain, that doesn't give me permission to close myself off and make him pay with my silent, self-righteous anger. Sure, in an ideal world, Steve, as the leader, would always be quick to repent and come after me when I retreat. But surprise! Like me, Steve is not perfect, and it usually doesn't work that way.

Now, when I am tempted to nurse my wounds, I try to remember the verse that says, "But when you are tempted, God will give you a way out so that you can stand up under it" (1 Corinthians 10:13 NIRV). It's true! God always throws me a life preserver: that not-so-subtle nudging that prompts me to set aside my pride, go to Steve, and say, "Let's talk about this."

When I do, my heavenly Father, like most dads, reminds me that life isn't fair and that the Christian life certainly isn't about getting what I think I deserve or being right. God is not as concerned with my happiness as He is in using the inevitable stresses of marriage to make me more like His Son. Ironically, dying to myself, or sacrificing my own desires to serve God and others, is the quickest way to find the abundant life God promises. The ultimate example of this is Jesus, who laid down His rights and His life.

. . . .

Speaking
mom-ese

How do you usually respond during an argument with your spouse? Do you vent? Retreat? How does God want you to react? Plan ahead how you will act the next time you are in the heat of an argument. Write down your strategy and follow through on your decision to respond with humility. _____

_____
_____
_____
_____
_____
_____
_____
_____
_____
_____
_____
_____
_____
_____
_____
_____
_____
_____
_____

Prayer

Dear Jesus, give me the strength You had when You laid down Your life for me. Help me to do the same for my husband. Help me to initiate reconciliation. After all, when I was yet a sinner, You died for me (see Romans 5:8).

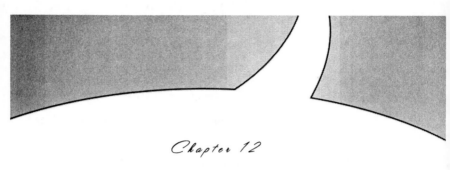

falling apart at the seams

· ·

**Because of the LORD's great love we are not
consumed, for his compassions never fail. They are
new every morning; great is your faithfulness.**

Lamentations 3:22–23 NIV

A dear neighbor was going through an excruciatingly painful season of life. One morning during my devotions, I read Psalm 102. I felt it spoke to my friend's situation so strongly that I needed to share it with her. She was a brand new believer, so along with relaying the *New King James Version*, I decided to share some of my thoughts about the passage. Under each verse, I wrote out my prayers for my friend:

Psalm 102:1–12 NKJV

vv. 1–2

"Hear my prayer, O LORD, and let my cry come to You. Do not hide Your face from me in the day of my trouble; incline Your ear to me; in the day that I call, answer me speedily."

My prayer: "I can't feel You, Lord. Are You listening? Please let me know that You can hear my heart crying out to You. Let me know that You care about what I'm going through. I know I can't presume upon You to listen to me. But in Your mercy, condescend to hear me. I can't make it much longer not knowing if You are even here. Please at least give me some indication that You are still here for me. I can't go on even another minute in this pain if I'm not assured that You are with me in the middle of it."

v. 3

"For my days are consumed like smoke, and my bones are burned like a hearth."

My prayer: "All I have ever accomplished has no value now. It has been proven to be so insubstantial that it has vaporized into thin air on this evil day. Even the framework of all that I thought was me—who I am at the most basic level—has been burned up by this trial."

v. 4

"My heart is stricken and withered like grass, so that I forget to eat my bread."

My prayer: "I am so sad that I have given up. I am not strong enough to face the heat of this time. Nothing brings me pleasure; I don't even feel like living. I am so consumed with my sorrow that nothing else matters. I can't even get up the gumption to spend time with You."

v. 5

"Because of the sound of my groaning my bones cling to my skin."

My prayer: "Because I am in such despair, there is nothing left except my spirit and my soul."

v. 6

"I am like a pelican of the wilderness; I am like an owl of the desert."

My prayer: "I have been searching for food and water where there is none. I have been looking for a place to rest, and yet there is no home for me."

v. 7

"I lie awake, and am like a sparrow alone on the housetop."

My prayer: "I am afraid. I feel so small and unprotected and removed from everything in life. Right now, no one would even think to come rescue me. I am unworthy to everyone but You, Lord. No one even sees me or gives me a second thought."

v. 8

"My enemies reproach me all day long; those who deride me swear an oath against me."

My prayer: "There is no rest from the people and circumstances that seek to destroy me. Even if I triumph for a moment, the outcome will ultimately be death."

vv. 9–10

"For I have eaten ashes like bread, and mingled my drink with weeping, because of Your indignation and Your wrath; for You have lifted me up and cast me away."

My prayer: "I feed on the memories of the good things that used to be in my life. And what I thirst for now is bittersweet, because I know even that will bring sadness. In my attempt to satisfy my longings, there is still pain. How could You do this to me? I believed in You because You have always taken care of me in the past. I have never been worthy before, so why have You chosen to punish me for my sins now? And the most severe punishment at that—separation from, and rejection by, You!"

v. 11

"My days are like a shadow that lengthens, and I wither away like grass."

My prayer: "My life is getting worse and worse, and I am getting weaker and weaker."

v. 12

"But You, O LORD, shall endure forever, and the remembrance of Your name to all generations."

My prayer: "But all this does not change the truth of Who

You are. I will fail. In fact, everything I thought was true will be destroyed. But that will not touch Your faithfulness, O God. You are the same Lord in the middle of all my hopelessness as You were yesterday in all my joy. Once I reach the other side of this battle, You will have been the only thing that has remained the same."

Have you ever felt like my neighbor or like King David, the original author of this psalm? Reread the last verse. It holds the key to holding on. Though everything around you may change, God will not. Though everything in your life may fall apart, God will remain a constant presence and support. If you are suffering, you may be full of questions. Take them to God; He is the answer. Just as David did so long ago, hold on to the Lord.

· ·

Speaking
mom-ese

Write down any of the areas in your life that seem to be falling apart at the seams. Now, make a confession of faith that in spite of your fears and concerns, you will trust God— even praise Him—in the middle of the storm. _____

_____
_____
_____
_____
_____
_____
_____
_____
_____
_____
_____
_____
_____
_____
_____
_____
_____
_____
_____

Prayer

God, I don't know if I can make it through this. It seems like more than I can handle. As an act of my will, however, I choose to believe that You have not deserted me but are right beside me, catching my tears and comforting me with Your Holy Spirit.

Chapter 13

prayer school

· ·

Draw near to God and He will draw near to you.

James 4:8a NASB

*O*ur family was in San Francisco to attend the Foursquare Denomination Convention, which Steve has produced for many years. The Lord often uses the convention to refine me—sometimes giving me correction, other times guiding me or providing prophetic impressions, encouragement, or a fresh revelation of an old truth. During this particular convention, God pressed in with a focus on prayer.

The first night I felt led to repent about my prayerlessness. It wasn't that I didn't pray. I simply felt the Lord calling me to a new level of communication with Him. I believe God understands the different seasons of a mother's life. He knew how hectic things had been for me, and for years He had been gracious about my sporadic prayers throughout the day. But now He wanted me to enter a new season, one for more extended times of prayer.

The truth is, God knew that my prayerlessness wasn't just the result of being a busy mom. I've always struggled with prayer; I just don't enjoy it. By nature, I would rather *do* something or even *talk* about doing something than bring up a subject over and over again. My reasoning is, *Lord, I've made my requests known to You. I've left them at Your feet, and I trust You to answer me. Why do I need to bring this up again?* Despite these frustrations, I'd always wanted to be a prayer warrior. I just wasn't able to pull myself up by my bootstraps enough to pray long and hard. So, time and again, I would confess my weakness in this area and ask God to teach me how to pray (and, I suppose, to give me the desire for prayer).

I returned home from San Francisco refreshed and ready to make a change. I made space in one of our closets, where I could sit on the floor in a place the kids couldn't easily find me, and there, I began to pray out loud. I knew that speaking audibly to God would make it more real for me, and it did. I also decided not to set my goals too high, committing at first to meet the Lord there for just five minutes a day. I knew He would inevitably meet me in my prayer closet, and that when He did, I would not want to leave so quickly. These little steps—what I came to think of as my own little prayer school—made a big difference in my prayer life. I still struggle with consistent prayer, and I probably always will, but the habits I began after San Francisco will stay with me always.

· ·

Speaking **mom-ese**

Describe the condition of your own prayer life. Then, if it's appropriate for the season in your life, write down ways you might be able to improve.

_____

_____
_____
_____
_____
_____
_____
_____
_____
_____
_____
_____
_____
_____
_____
_____

Prayer

Thank You, Lord, for the power of prayer. Please forgive me for the times I've taken this privilege for granted. Help me to follow through on the changes I need to make in order to draw closer to You. Help me to find specific times to pray so that I can maintain an ongoing life of communication and conversation with You.

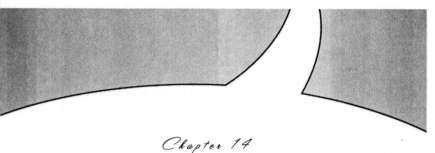

Chapter 14

put your hand in His hand

· ·

And your ears will hear a word behind you, "This is the way, walk in it," whenever you turn to the right or to the left.

Isaiah 30:21 NASB

Steve, the kids, and I were vacationing in the Northwest with our friend Bill and his family, and we had all decided to go on a hike. Before we started, we fortified ourselves with my favorite kind of breakfast—coffee and an assortment of cakes and pastries. Then we hit the trails, ready to explore Dee Wright Observatory in central Oregon.

The observatory is a castlelike structure surrounded by, and constructed with, lava rock, and it practically called out to Tucker, "Come climb me, little boy." I have to admit, it was magical. It looked just like the set of a prehistoric movie. With every brush of wind, I ducked in anticipation of a pterodactyl swooping past me to grab its prey. The surroundings even brought out the caveman in Steve. I wrote it off when he addressed me as "Woman," but I drew the line when he tried to grab me by the hair and pull me behind a lava rock!

Our next stop was Proxy Falls, where my nature-loving husband was on his cell phone until we hiked out of range. It was a good thing Steve lost reception, because after the first mile, he was ready to call in a helicopter tour to come pick him up. Despite the long hike, though, I think he was glad he had hung up the phone. The falls were spectacular.

I love Oregon! I thought happily. *No wonder old hippies never die—they just move to the Northwest.* Unfortunately, on our way to our next destination, Sahalie Falls, we saw one of them in all his glory. As we came around the corner, Mr. Hippie was getting dressed after a dip in the McKenzie River. Haven got quite the eyeful—giving her one memory from our vacation that she would like to forget! She begged Bill to go beat him up, reasoning, "He abused us with his nakedness." I just shook my head, wondering how a nine-year-old girl could sound like a bad romance novel when she'd never even read one. Silently praying over Haven, I asked the Lord to overexpose that picture in her mind by shining the light of Jesus on it.

Each destination was more breathtaking—and memorable—than the next. My favorite part of the whole day however was the journey. Hiking the trail behind Bill and his three-year-old daughter, Marissa, I reflected on the father-heart of God. Sometimes Bill carried his little girl; other times he simply held her hand. Occasionally he let her walk alone, but he never let go of her with his eyes. All along the way he provided encouragement, saying, "You can do it," or "You're a good little hiker," as if he were noticing for the first time. "Oh, Daddy," Marissa would protest, "you always say that! And you always say I'm smart, too."

Our heavenly Father is like that. He cheers us on and tells us we can make it, supporting us when we're tired or scared or want to give up. That's one of the reasons I like to read my Bible every day. I like to hear my Father tell me over and over that I can make it to the end of my journey. And I know that I will, because He constantly guides me, reminding me when to hold His hand, when to let Him carry me, and when to enjoy being the apple of His eye.

. . . .

Speaking mom-ese

Do you need some guidance today?
Take hold of Your Father's hand and
let Him lead you. If you're anxious
about your path, tell God your
concerns. Ask Him questions about
where you're headed. Then open His
Word and wait for His encouragement
and leading. _____

_____

_____

_____

_____

_____

_____

_____

_____

_____

_____

_____

_____

_____

_____

_____

Prayer

*Father, I know that I want to follow You, but I'm afraid that sometimes I get
ahead of You or let go of Your hand to go my own way. Help me to stand still
and wait for You to find me, take my hand, and lead me on the right path.
Thank You, Abba.*

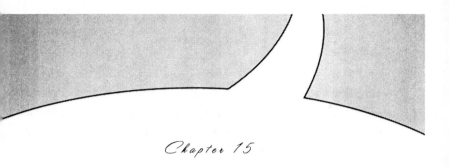

in God we trust

. . . .

First pay attention to me, and then relax. Now you can take it easy—you're in good hands.

Proverbs 1:33 MSG

had just returned home from a busy speaking tour. When I unloaded my suitcase, though, I discovered that I had misplaced my laptop computer. I began to pray fervently while Steve fired up the minivan and rushed me back to the airport. On the way, I called the airport's lost and found department, but they didn't have any record of a missing laptop. Then I called the airport police, but they hadn't seen it, either. The security guards connected me to my airline's baggage claim office.

"Oh, you must be Alcorn," the airline representative said.

I sighed in relief. "No, I'm not Alcorn, but you must have my computer because I had Mr. Alcorn's phone number on my laptop." I thanked the lady and the Lord profusely. The airline had found the lost laptop way back in Philadelphia, one of the many stopovers on my speaking tour.

When Steve and I got home, I called my friend Randy Alcorn, assuming he had gotten a phone call from the nice people at the airline. Randy had already contacted me via e-mail to tell me where to find my computer . . . and also to share the funny conversation he'd had with the baggage claim lady. Here is Randy's e-mail:

Lisa,

By any chance did you leave a bag at the Philadelphia airport that has a Bible or Christian book in it and an IBM Think Pad? I just got a Twilight Zone-like call, saying that I had left my bag in Philly. I said, "I don't think so. Haven't been there for a while."

"But we have your IBM ThinkPad."

"Good. But I don't have an IBM ThinkPad."

"Well, tell us some identifying files just to make sure, then we'll ship it to you."

"Can't give you any identifying files for a computer I don't own."

"Okay. Do you have a Bible?"

"Sure. It's right here."

"Maybe this isn't a Bible. Do you have a Christian book?"

"Yep. Lots of them."

"Well, we've got your name right here. Are you sure you're Randy Alcorn?"

"Positive. Have been all my life."

"Is your phone number _____?"

"The one you just called? Yes. I'm right here."

Well, this went on for a while, and I was dying laughing at the whole exchange. Then I said, "Can you find any other names?"

"We can't find a name on the bag."

"How about in the Think Pad?"

So she searched for a while and finally said, "How about Tucker? Haven? Clancy?"

I said, "I've got a friend who has kids with those names. And I recently e-mailed her my phone numbers."

"You sure this isn't yours, though?"

"If I had kids named Tucker, Haven, and

Clancy, I would know."

"I suppose so. But are you sure it's your friend's?"

"Either that or someone else's with kids named Tucker, Haven, and Clancy."

"Could be."

"Probably not. I'll contact my friend."

I asked them to be sure it would be completely safe until I could check with you. They said they'd keep it there safely for thirty days. So here's the number to call at the Philly airport: _____.

Hope this works for you. If they don't let you claim it (since they insist it's mine—after all, my name and phone number is in there!), I'll call back and have them ship it to me, and then I'll ship to you. Hopefully it won't come to that. :) It's been fun, sis. I'll never forget that conversation. Made my day.

Investing in eternity,

Randy Alcorn

Don't you know that some of the panicky conversations we have with God are just as entertaining to Him as this conversation was to Randy? I can just imagine the number of times I've been frantically praying about something, and God has simply been sitting back, with a big grin on His face, knowing He has already worked out a plan. When you are tempted to panic, remember this verse: "While we look not at the things which are seen, but at the things which are not seen; for the things which are seen are temporal, but the things which are not seen are eternal" (2 Corinthians 4:18 NASB).

. . . .

Speaking
mom-ese

In God we trust? You bet! One of the most important lessons we can ever learn is to trust God for everything— not some things, not most things, but for everything. List the important parts of your life that you need to entrust to Him. Now stop scrambling to make it all work out on your own, and instead, rest in the knowledge that God is already working it out in His way and His time. _____

_____
_____
_____
_____
_____
_____
_____
_____
_____
_____
_____
_____
_____
_____
_____
_____

Prayer

I know I must crack You up with some of my panicky prayers, Father. Help me to trust You more and to remember that You have everything under control. Help me resist trying to control things myself. I place my life safely in Your capable hands.

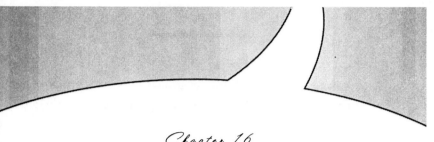

Chapter 16

the Lord is my daddy

· ·

He said to them, "But who do you say that I am?"

Matthew 16:15 NKJV

*O*ne of the most memorable and powerful Bible studies I have done is one by T. W. Hunt. In his book, *Disciple's Prayer Life*, the author uses exercises to help readers understand how each relationship with God is unique. After listing the many names and titles of God recorded in the Bible, he explains that the name we call someone often identifies our relationship with that person: for example, "daddy" (child), "doctor" (patient), "teacher" (student), and "honey" (lover). He then asks readers to reflect on their own relationship with God and identify the most common role they assume with the Lord. Some examples he provides are worker to boss, hiker to guide, team member to coach, crew member to captain, musician to conductor, servant to master, subject to king, citizen to president, and so on. The last step in the exercise is to personalize Psalm 23 from your own perspective, using the relationship you identified as your unique prayer identity with God.

After much thought, I realized that at that time in my life, I most often thought of my relationship with God as "empty vessel" to "the source." This is how my personal psalm came out.

The Lord is my source;

I shall not rely on myself.

He leads me to empty myself out before Him;

He makes me clean because of His blood.

He restores the gifts within me;

He leads me to be filled with His Spirit.

Yes, though I walk through impossible situations,

I will not be afraid; I will choose to believe.

I will put my trust in Your power and mercy.

You prepare eternal work for me to do;

You anoint me for the task;

Your glory flows in and through me!

Surely Your name will be praised forever,

And I will humbly cast my crown at Your feet in worship!

I also often relate to God as my father. In fact, I entitled my
autobiography, *The Facts of Life and Other Lessons My Father
Taught Me*, because although I have a great dad, it was my heavenly Father who taught me the majority of life's most important
lessons. I love being His little girl. I believe that this relationship touches most women in the depths of their heart. From this
perspective, I wrote another Psalm 23.

The Lord is my Daddy,

I will be loved and adored.

I crawl up into His lap

and am safely wrapped in His arms.

I lay my head against His heart

and find rest for my mind, body, and soul.

I learn to trust.

I take His hand; He holds mine,

and we walk together through my life.

Surely I will face fear, hurt,

disappointment, and loss,

but You are bigger than any

ugly monster hiding under my bed.

I will not be afraid of the Dark,
because You are the Light.

I don't even think about tomorrow,
what I will eat, wear, or where I will live,
because You are my Abba.
I don't need to worry;
You will take good care of me—
I am your little girl!

You are the Father of my future,
and You have blessings and hope planned for me.
You enjoy giving me good gifts.
I make You smile when I dance
with giddy thanksgiving in Your presence.

Speaking mom-ese

Now you try it. Think of how you usually relate to God and identify the most common relationship you assume with Him. Now, stretch beyond your comfort zone and try your hand at writing your own Psalm 23.

_____
_____
_____
_____
_____
_____
_____
_____
_____
_____
_____
_____
_____
_____
_____
_____
_____
_____
_____

Prayer

Thank You, God, that You created us to be in relationship with You. I want to experience the fullness of relationship with You as my teacher, father, Lord, savior, healer, encourager, and everything in between. I'm so glad I get to have a bond with You for eternity.

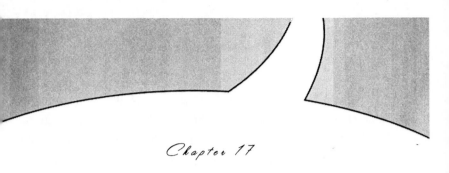

Chapter 17

no pain, no gain

. . . .

**Children, obey your parents in all things:
for this is wellpleasing unto the Lord.**

Colossians 3:20 KJV

*H*aven was having a bad day. She was utterly argumentative, infinitely disrespectful, and indefensibly defiant. (Am I making my point?) Steve and I warned her that if she continued to dispute everything we said, we would have to take drastic measures. Simply talking about her poor attitude wasn't changing her behavior.

Sure enough, Haven kept it up. So I sat her down and said, "Haven, I want you to prepare yourself for some serious consequences. Because you have refused to listen to warnings, you will not be allowed to have Tessa spend the night this weekend!"

Haven burst into tears. She was heartbroken, but we soon saw that her *spirit* was not. The next day, she began arguing again. I warned Haven that the next thing to go would be her bowling class on Tuesday. She continued to push the boundaries of respectfulness, so Steve and I had to follow through and tell Haven that bowling was out. Again, she cried, this time explaining that if she didn't bowl two games before next week, she couldn't qualify for an upcoming tournament. She whined and yelled and cried some more, but we didn't relent.

When I put her to bed that night, she was still crying. "Mom," she finally admitted to me, "I don't know why I argue so much. When I do, I know that I'm going to get in trouble, but I just want to prove to you that I can get my own way and that I'm stronger than you. I want to stop but I can't. Then when you correct me, I get so angry that I just want to run away."

I pulled her close. "Haven, do you remember the two girls who were prisoners of the Taliban during the 9/11 crisis?" I asked. "The United States sent its allies into Afghanistan to rescue the girls, and they were brought home safely. But what if the girls fought against the soldiers who were sent to bring them home because they didn't believe the men were truly on their side? The soldiers would have had to physically carry them out of the prison, and the girls probably would have gotten bruised in the process.

"Or what if the girls had threatened to break free and run

away from the soldiers?" I continued, "The soldiers probably would have needed to tie them up and subdue them so they could be transported to freedom."

I stroked her tear-stained face and explained, "God has sent us as your parents to protect you from potential bondage. But instead of trusting that we are here to help you, you fight us. When you do that, Daddy and I have to hold you closer. We won't let go, because we know what's best for you, but often in the process you get hurt. And the more you fight, the more we have to clamp down and restrict you from certain freedoms.

"All you have to do is believe that we are on your side," I told her. "If you will simply trust us, you will find the freedom that comes through submitting to authority."

It's a tough concept for our kids to understand—that freedom comes with rules and discipline. But it's important that they learn to grasp that truth and that we, as parents, follow through on implementing rules and consequences. I truly believe that, as parents, we are put here on earth to protect and guide our children. Of course, it's not fun or easy to dispense such correction; to be honest, I constantly second-guess my parenting choices. But then I remind myself that it's better for us to discipline our children today if we hope to prevent the world from dispensing its own form of punishment tomorrow.

. . . .

Make a note of any areas you need to toughen up a bit with your children. Why have you loosened up? How can you turn things around?_____

_____

_____
_____
_____
_____
_____
_____
_____
_____
_____
_____
_____
_____
_____
_____
_____
_____
_____
_____
_____

Prayer

Lord, give me the strength to be firm with my kids when I need to be. Help me to draw safe boundaries for them, and then give me the fortitude to maintain those boundaries. Help my children to see that I love them, even when they don't understand my means of expressing it. Thank You for providing me with an example of how to correct my children.

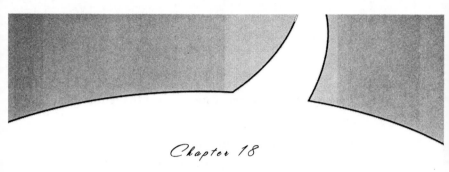

Chapter 18

land of the free...
gift with purchase

· ·

**Then he said, "Beware! Don't be greedy for
what you don't have. Real life is not measured
by how much we own."**

Luke 12:15 NLT

We were at the largest shopping center in the United States—
the Mall of America in Minneapolis, Minnesota. Wow! You've
got to see this place to believe it. In the center of the mall is
Camp Snoopy, an amusement park complete with roller coasters
and a log ride. The theme park is anchored by large department
stores like Nordstrom, Sears, Bloomingdales, and Macy's. Sand-
wiched in between are more than four hundred specialty stores
along with attractions that include a bowling alley, a world-class
aquarium, the LEGO Imagination Center, the NASCAR Silicon
Motor Speedway, restaurants, movie theaters, and more, more,

more. The place truly gives new meaning to the phrase "shop till you drop!"

Before we set out, Steve and I gave our kids careful instructions—well, some people might call them threats: "Don't touch, don't ask, don't wander, don't whine, don't complain, don't yell, don't run, don't dawdle, and most of all, have a great time." Then, when we had made things perfectly clear, Steve, the children, and I went to explore the great indoors. The sights and sounds of this shopper's paradise immediately bombarded our senses. Yep, the Mall of America, the mother of all malls, is indeed the land of the free ... gift with purchase.

As we passed store after store, I was reminded that the United States is a nation of shoppers. Yet even we as Christians are tempted by materialism. We often misread spiritual yearnings as natural cravings. Some of us try to fill up this emptiness with food, others with fun, many with work, but there is something especially fulfilling about spending money. It's easy to believe that if we buy those adorable shoes, or fabulous dress, or darling knick-knack, it will satisfy us. Like all other fleshly indulgences, however, buying stuff leaves us broke. (And I'm not just talking about our bank accounts.)

Money in and of itself is not evil—the *love* of money is. Let's face facts. Earthly possessions are totally, completely, and unalterably temporary. Everything in the Mall of America (except for the souls of the believers who happen to be there) can be categorized as "here today and gone tomorrow." Our spiritual riches, however, are permanent. They are ours today, ours tomorrow, ours for eternity!

There's absolutely nothing for sale at the mall that can offer you earthly peace and eternal salvation. So, here's your challenge and mine. The next time you feel bored or lonely or depressed, don't go shopping. You may feel better temporarily, but the high will wear off and the new shoes will wear out. Instead, spend your time and money investing in something that will last, something eternal. Give yourself away by serving the Lord. Contrary to popular opinion, the dollar is not almighty—God is!

. . . .

Speaking
mom-ese

Take an honest assessment of your life
and determine whether there is anything or anyone you are looking for
satisfaction from other than Jesus.
Here's a clue. Would you be willing
to give that person or item up if God
asked you to in order to devote more of
your time and attention to Him? Make a list of areas that
you want to completely surrender to God._____

_____

_____

_____

_____

_____

_____

_____

_____

_____

_____

_____

_____

_____

_____

_____

Prayer

*Jesus, I know that only You can really satisfy my heart's desires.
Please forgive me when I look to modern day idols like clothes, cars, and
houses rather than You. Teach me how to abide in You. Fill me with Your
Spirit so that I'm too content to look anywhere else for temporary and
artificial pleasure. I want to desire only You.*

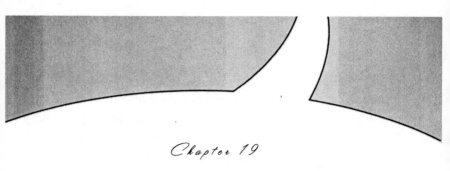

how does God
measure worth?

· ·

**'Come, you who are blessed by my Father;
take your inheritance, the kingdom prepared for
you since the creation of the world.... I tell you the
truth, whatever you did for one of the least of these
brothers of mine, you did for me.'**

Matthew 25:34b,40b NIV

I'm very proud of my mother. She is an amazing woman who
can succeed at whatever she puts her mind to. She has been an
executive secretary, city council member, Girl Scout leader, soft-
ball coach, PTA president, top residential real estate agent, and
now, she's closing deals right and left in commercial real estate.

As successful as my mom has been in the workplace, her
crowning achievements have been at home. She has poured 110

percent of her heart, soul, and mind into raising her three kids, and her efforts have paid off. All three of us are happy, healthy adults who strive to make a positive difference in the world. Through her children, my mother will continue to impact this earth—and God's kingdom—for eternity.

Her influence extends beyond her own kids, though. My mom is also (in my totally unbiased opinion) the best grandmother who ever lived. My kids call her every day to talk about their lives, complain about me, cry on her shoulder, and ask for her advice. She is happily teaching another generation with her godly wisdom and her unconditional love.

For several years, my mother juggled living in two different states in order to help take care of her own mother. She worked long hours in Texas selling real estate to help prepare for their retirement years, caring for her elderly mother, "Nanny," while she was there. Then she flew back to California at least twice a month to rejoin her husband and college-age son, Casey. In the middle of all that juggling, she learned the inevitability of dropping a few balls. Fortunately, she had the wisdom to know which ones to let fall to the ground. The one ball she never let drop was the time she spent with Nanny. No matter how busy things got, my mom always made time to take her on day trips or garage sale excursions. She also stopped in at my grandmother's house each day to play dominoes or watch *The Wheel*.

We are all busy. We are all balancing multiple responsibilities. The question is, are we cramming in the "important" things at the expense of the eternal?

Whose scales are you using to balance your priorities—God's or the world's?

• •

Speaking mom-ese

Is there someone in your family who deserves a little more of your time? If so, write that person's name below and identify a few ways you can spend more time with him or her.

_____

_____
_____
_____
_____
_____
_____
_____
_____
_____
_____
_____
_____
_____

Prayer
Lord, show me how to serve You by serving others. When I get caught up in the busyness of life, gently remind me to stop and touch someone's life with Your love. Help me to prioritize my time with Your desires in mind.

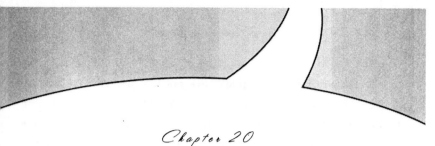

the covering of family

. . . .

**Every beast, every creeping thing, and every bird,
everything that moves on the earth, went out by
their families from the ark.**

Genesis 8:19 NASB

*E*very holiday I say the same thing: I am so sick of eating! After all the feasting, I usually feel like Haven, who once remarked after a wonderful meal, "I don't think I have enough skin to keep my stomach all in." And if feeling bloated isn't enough to remind me to watch my ham and turkey intake, I always have the words of my youngest daughter, Clancy. One holiday weekend, she asked if she could walk with me in the morning. I told her that I probably wouldn't be walking as much anymore because it was getting too cold. "Oh yeah," she replied. "To keep warm this winter you will need the extra blubber."

Fortunately, the holidays are not just about food, they are about family. Looking back on seasons past, some of my best memories come from the many nights my extended family spent playing games—especially "spades" with my partner, Haven, the card shark! I'll also never forget my sister-in-law, Cindy's, Green Velvet Cake (the store was out of red food coloring). I still chuckle under my breath thinking about the year Steve repeatedly called his brother Tim "Tucker" and Tucker "Tim." (Doesn't that always happen at family gatherings?) And I loved watching Tim's expression as Tucker opened up the early Christmas gift that Tim bought for his nephew: a remote control monster truck. I don't know who had more fun playing with that thing, Uncle Tim or Tucker.

Another mental snapshot I have is of Grandpa sitting in his favorite rocking chair, laughing good-naturedly as the kids would say, "Grandpa Rocks!" I don't have a snapshot of Grandma, though; she moves so fast that my mental image of her is more like a video. Each holiday she bustles about, cooking in the kitchen, folding laundry, taking care of Steve's mentally disabled sister Kathy, or working on some project.

When I think about how grateful I am to God for the privilege of having—and marrying into—such a happy, healthy family, I picture the awning on our motor home. On trips, we used it for protection against both the heat and the rain. Isn't that how it is with family, too? When life's problems begin to heat up or troubles seem to rain down on us, it is good to be able to find comfort in the love of family.

You may be thinking, "I don't have the kind of family you have, Lisa. My family is dysfunctional and scattered and certainly doesn't offer protection and comfort." Maybe so, but I want to encourage you to reconsider that statement. Instead, picture an awning that is tattered and ripped to shreds. It is old, barely functioning, and is definitely more holey than holy. Wouldn't this awning—while flawed—still offer more shade than if you were standing out in the heat uncovered? Wouldn't this awning—while full of holes—still provide you with enough protection to avoid getting drenched?

Every family has great big tears in its fabric. You've gotta trust me, mine isn't perfect either! But let's learn to thank God for the covering of family, despite what kind of shape it is in. Stepping under that protective umbrella sure is better than facing the world alone.

. . . .

Speaking
mom-ese

Who put the holes in the covering of your family? Will you forgive him or her? Are you willing to stop examining the holes in your family and instead ask God to restore wholeness? Jot down a few names, pray for God to bring redemption, and look for ways to restore those relationships._____

_____

_____

_____

_____

_____

_____

_____

_____

_____

_____

_____

_____

_____

_____

_____

Prayer

Lord, forgive me for holding grudges and standing out in the rain, rather than extending forgiveness to those in my family who have let me down. Cover our family with Your wings and draw us closer to You and subsequently, to each other.

clothe me in righteousness

· ·

**Walk as children of Light (for the fruit of the Light
consists in all goodness and righteousness and
truth), trying to learn what is pleasing to the Lord.
Do not participate in the unfruitful deeds of dark-
ness, but instead even expose them.**

Ephesians 5:8–11 NASB

I had a wonderful time filming *The Facts of Life Reunion*
movie, and I loved the wardrobe I got to wear as the spoiled,
rich girl, "Blair." When the filming came to a close, I tried hard
to negotiate to either buy the clothes or receive them for free.
Over and over again I got the same negative answer. In the past,
actors had been known to beg for their movie wardrobes, only to
sell them later at a premium. So now the studio had drawn the
line. Nobody was allowed to keep his or her wardrobe.

I was disappointed. As a longtime stay-at-home mom, I never
had any reason to go out and buy expensive, designer clothes.

But I knew that soon we were going to start doing media interviews—and I would need some nice outfits to wear for the cameras.

On the last night of filming, the wardrobe lady came up with a great idea. She suggested that I go out and buy a less expensive black suit and bring it to her several days later. She would exchange it for the fancy black suit that had been tailored specifically for me. This sounded terrific, so soon after, I went to the nearest department store and found a cheap black suit. I also found a similar pink shirt, blue shirt, and gray jacket to exchange. This way I would have two complete outfits.

I took a cab over to the production company later that afternoon and made the switch. That night, however, as I lay awake praying, God brought to mind the issue of the suits. He reminded me of the many times I have told my children, "Deception is lying with our actions instead of our words." He also made me realize that if I wore those outfits on an interview show, my castmates Kimmie and Mindy would surely recognize them from the movie. They had wanted to buy some of their wardrobe as well. How would I explain the fact that I got some of my outfits and they didn't? That would certainly put the wardrobe department in a bad position. Once the secret was out, there would be nothing I could tell them to justify my actions and redeem my testimony as a woman of faith. Of course, that should have been my first hint. Anytime we have to do something in the dark, it usually means that it won't stand up to the light.

The next day, I packed up the suits and shirts and sent them back to the production office. I told the costumer to feel free to give the clothes I exchanged to charity or to take them back to the store and give the money away. The lesson ended up costing me a few hundred dollars, but it would have cost me a whole lot more if I had gotten away with it. Making the right choice was better than any feeling I would have gotten from wearing the most expensive, designer suit.

. . . .

Speaking
mom-ese

Are there any gray areas in your life?
Expose them to the light. Make note
of those shadowy spots where you
want Jesus to shine His light. Then
allow Him to uncover any deception
the enemy has attempted to hide
from you. _____

_____

_____

_____

_____

_____

_____

_____

_____

_____

_____

_____

_____

_____

_____

_____

_____

_____

Prayer
"Search me, O God, and know my heart; test me and know my anxious
thoughts. See if there is any offensive way in me, and lead me in the way
everlasting" (Psalm 139:23–24 NIV).

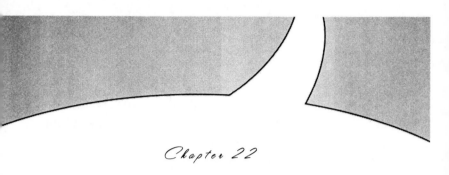

Chapter 22

if the shoe fits

. . . .

**For shoes, put on the peace that comes from the
Good News, so that you will be fully prepared.**

Ephesians 6:15 NLT

It was dark outside and too early for anyone to be getting up. But I had to arise at 5:00 a.m. in order to make the two-hour drive to the airport. I quietly showered, got dressed, and packed without waking the rest of my family. Once I finished, I woke Steve with the smell of fresh, hot coffee, and we carried the kids to the car wrapped in their blankets, buckling them in gently so as not to interrupt their dreams. We always look forward to having a car of sleeping kids, because Steve and I love to talk on long car rides. The commute goes by more quickly. When we arrived at the airport, I kissed my sleeping babies—and my big baby—and waved goodbye with promises of more kisses the following night.

I wheeled my suitcase into the busy airport, ready to board the plane to Colorado Springs, where I was scheduled to appear on a *Focus on the Family* broadcast with Dr. James Dobson the following day. Still groggy, I walked through the sliding airport doors, scraping my heel against the sidewalk in an attempt to dislodge a rock from my left shoe. It didn't work, so I reached down to pick whatever it was off the bottom. Aside from a small kitten heel, nothing was there. *Oh my goodness,* I realized, *the heel must have come off my other shoe.* Bending down, I grasped the bottom of my right foot. Bingo! As I'd suspected, there was no heel.

Suddenly my face reddened. My right shoe was flat, all right, but it never had a heel. in the first place. I had been hobbling down the airport corridor wearing two different shoes! It was easy to see how it had happened. Both shoes were black, but one was heeled and the other a flat. *This is bad,* I told myself. I looked down again. One shoe had a cloth toe, the other a leather toe. *This is very bad.*

Of course, in an attempt to travel light, I hadn't packed any other shoes. So I was forced to walk peg-legged to the gate and hobble through a transfer in Denver before finally arriving in the Colorado Springs airport. Thank the Lord for Wal-Marts! My first stop after picking up the rental car was at the superstore, where I bought a pair of $7.88 black flats in 8-wide. And I don't mind telling the whole world that I was never so happy to put on a pair of shoes in my life.

Walking with mismatched shoes and dealing with the physical imbalance that can ensue is difficult (especially when you're trying to catch a flight!). But walking successfully through life when you're *spiritually* imbalanced—that is, lacking direction from God—is impossible. When I think about traveling along the Bible's narrow path, I am reminded of the Old Testament verse that says, "Whether you turn to the right or to the left, your ears will hear a voice behind you, saying, 'This is the way; walk in it'" (Isaiah 30:21 NIV). If you want to live a balanced life, led by God, then you must listen for His direction and be ready to move.

• •

Speaking
mom-ese

Are any areas of your life out of
balance? Do you feel anxious or ill-
equipped for travel? If so, note any
choices you might be making that
are throwing your spiritual life out
of whack. Then ask God to lead you in
the way you should walk. _____

_____

_____

_____

_____

_____

_____

_____

_____

_____

_____

_____

_____

_____

_____

_____

_____

_____

Prayer
Lord, lead me in Your way and give me peace that I am walking in Your
footsteps. If any area of my life is unbalanced, show me what changes I need
to make in order to walk in sync with You.

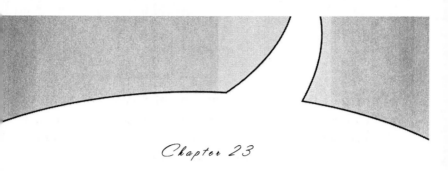

the story of the stinky suit

· ·

**Therefore I tell you, do not worry about your life,
what you will eat or drink; or about your body,
what you will wear. Is not life more important than
food, and the body more important than clothes?**

Matthew 6:25 NIV

This wasn't just any old radio interview, so I started the day early, about 5 a.m. I needed plenty of time to get ready, both physically and spiritually. I showered and quickly climbed back into my pajamas so I could put off squeezing into pantyhose, dress shoes, and professional wear until the last possible moment. Then, once I'd fixed my face and my hair, I turned my focus to my heart. I knew it was going to be an important day, and the last thing I needed to do was attempt it on my own strength. It sounds contradictory, but I spent the next thirty minutes alternately petitioning the Lord in detail for my heart's desires and then asking Him to erase my agenda and let His will triumph.

Finally, I put on my purple uniform (the outfit I always wear when I need to look nice, but can get away with not wearing a dress). As I donned the outfit I noticed a musty smell, but I put it out of my mind and rushed out the door.

When I got in the car, the odor intensified. I thought perhaps it had rained overnight and I had left the windows down in the car, but they were tightly shut. When I met my manager, Ron, the first thing I did was ask if he smelled anything funny. "Yeah," he replied, "and I think it's you!" I sniffed the sleeve of my jacket and ... yuck. There was a definite moldy smell saturating my favorite outfit.

It was then that I realized why my suit smelled like it had been soaked in mold-water. My suitcase had gotten wet the week before and had been sitting in standing water for several days. Sure, my luggage had dried out before I packed my clothes, but it still retained a mildew smell that had transferred directly to my purple uniform. I was stuck in some very stinky clothes. It was too late to run to the store and get a new outfit, and I couldn't cancel my "Doctor's appointment," as in my interview with Dr. James Dobson!

I was already nervous about meeting Dr. Dobson, but fortunately, my apprehension disappeared as soon as he extended his hand and greeted me in that familiar, reassuring voice that I've heard hundreds of times. Thankfully, I was being interviewed on his radio show so the audience couldn't smell me. And Dr. Dobson either had a stuffy nose that day or he was too polite to mention the stench. Either way, the stinky suit was a non-issue and my radio appearance turned out to be the memory of a lifetime.

When I returned home that night I began to wonder, *What was that all about? Was there something I was supposed to learn by smelling like a Petri dish on this very important day?* You know what? I don't think there was. I think life just sometimes throws us curveballs. We can either quickly adjust and use them to our advantage, or we can let them pass us by without taking a swing. It's not worth making a big deal out of life's hassles and headaches. In the bigger scheme of things, most of the things that get us all upset aren't really worth the stress. And often, as in the case with my stinky suit, what is consuming to us isn't even noticed by others.

Worry buys us nothing. So don't get all worked up over life's inevitable bumps in the road. The Bible says there is a time to laugh and a time to cry (see Ecclesiastes 3:4). If you have a choice, laugh about it.

. . . .

Speaking
mom-ese

Write down the things you are
stressed about today. Now picture
yourself placing these things in
God's big, powerful, able, and
loving hands. Leave them there.
Throughout the day, as little inconven-
iences attempt to steal your joy, make the choice to laugh
in the face of them. _____

_____

_____

_____

_____

_____

_____

_____

_____

_____

_____

_____

_____

_____

_____

_____

_____

_____

Prayer

Lord, help me to have Your perspective. When I am tempted to make a moun-
tain out of a molehill or cry when I could laugh, remind me that
You are in control. Give me a sense of humor about life's little problems.

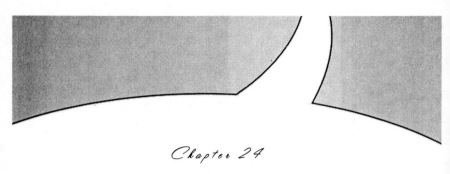

to love and honor

. . . .

**Nevertheless let each one of you in particular so
love his own wife as himself, and let the wife see
that she respects her husband.**

Ephesians 5:33 NKJV

*T*raffic was horrible, and I was late for a book signing at a
bookstore. It was the Friday before Christmas, and the store
was located in a high-volume shopping district. We were running about ten minutes late, and I could just imagine people
waiting in line for me, wondering if I was ever going to show up.
Steve called the bookstore owners to assure them I was on my
way, but my stomach was in knots—our minivan was crawling
down the street at a pace so slow, it seemed as if we were moving
backward.

When the bookstore came into sight, I asked Steve if I could just hop out of our van and run across the street while he found a parking space. He said no, that he wanted to pull up to the curb and drop me off. I tried to be patient, but it seemed ridiculous to make those book-buying customers wait when I could simply dash across the street. So I voiced my frustrations until Steve finally said, "Fine, go!"

I ran over to the bookstore, but Steve never came in. He took the kids to grab some lunch and then picked me up when it was over. (Do I need to mention that he was ticked?) Later that evening, he looked at me and said, "You know that I'm still mad at you, don't you?" I had to admit that Steve's feelings were obvious . . . *extremely* obvious.

When I asked Steve why he was still angry, he confessed, "Because you didn't let me take care of you." When he said that, it felt as if someone had opened a window and let a blast of winter air in. I immediately realized I had been wrong. I had mistakenly believed that by considering the needs of the customers in the bookstore, I was doing the right thing. Instead, I should have shown my husband respect by trusting his judgment and letting him drop me off at the curb. Had I done so, I might have been a few more minutes late, but I would have honored Steve.

Why do we so often put strangers—and their feelings—ahead of our loved ones? Perhaps it's because we sometimes take our loved ones for granted. But our family members should be treated with the utmost respect. So the next time you're tempted to treat anyone in your family like a second-class citizen, think again. Also if you're lucky enough to have a husband who takes pride in taking care of you, let him.

· ·

Speaking
m o m - e s e

Make a list of some practical ways you can show respect to your husband, children, family, and friends.

_____

_____

_____
_____
_____
_____
_____
_____
_____
_____
_____
_____
_____
_____
_____
_____
_____
_____

Prayer
Lord, please forgive me for the times I put strangers before my own family.
Help me to show them not just love but also respect. Teach me how to do this
in practical ways.

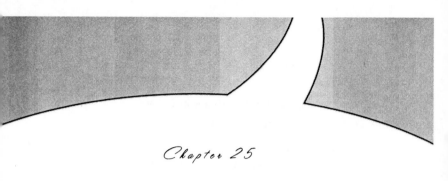

mother of a teenager

· ·

**A wise son heeds his father's instruction, but a
mocker does not listen to rebuke.**

Proverbs 13:1 NIV

Yikes, I said to myself as I faced one of motherhood's great
divides. *I'm about to become the mother of a teenager!* Tucker's
thirteenth birthday was just around the corner, which was a big
deal to Tucker, but an even bigger deal to me. I don't think it was
a coincidence that my eyes started having trouble focusing two
days after the birthday party. I'm sure bifocals are next.

Steve and I had been preparing Tucker for this milestone
for many months. We wanted him to understand that this wasn't
just any old birthday—this was his transition from childhood to
young adulthood. In the week leading up to the big day, we told

him that his days to behave like a kid were almost over. Believe me, he played it for all it was worth.

On the morning of Tucker's birthday, we had a family celebration around the breakfast table. I'd planned to have the party at Tucker's favorite pancake house, but he was mortified at the thought of opening gifts in public, so we opted for coffee and bagels at home. I attached an envelope to each of his gifts explaining what the present represented for this exciting new season of his life.

The last gift was the announcement that he would be taking a weekend trip with his dad to San Francisco. On the drive to San Francisco and back, the two of them listened to all six of Dr. James Dobson's *Preparing for Adolescence* tapes. These cassettes cover all of the questions that kids Tucker's age need answered, such as peer pressure, sexuality, hormones, body changes, and relationships.

Tucker hated every minute of those tapes. At one point he called me on Steve's cell phone and whispered, "Help! Get me out of here!" He even asked Steve, "Why are you torturing me by making me listen to this stuff?" Steve explained that it was important for Tucker to hear accurate information, and that he needed to hear that information in an environment where he could talk things over with his dad. Steve acknowledged that Tucker wasn't facing most of these issues yet, but there would come a time when he would. The pep talk must have made a difference because Steve reported that Tucker stopped pretending like he was about to jump out of the car.

Once the guys arrived in San Francisco, they focused on having fun. They walked around town, ate delicious food, enjoyed the hotel, and stumbled onto their own little piece of heaven—the Sony Center. Steve spent hours checking out the latest in high tech toys while Tucker played all of the Play Station 2 games on giant flat screen panels.

Something happened that weekend. Maybe it was Dr. Dobson's tapes, the time with Dad, or both, but Tucker came home different. The change probably had more to do with the way we were treating him—like a young man.

If you are facing a milestone birthday or experience with your kids, I encourage you to make it a special time. Celebrate it! Be intentional about telling them what you want them to get from the experience. Like Tucker, they may pretend to hate every minute of your "lecture," but your words and the experience will stay with them.

· ·

Speaking
mom-ese

Make a list of the significant things you
need to talk to your children about.
Then begin making preparations for
those conversations. _____

_____

_____
_____
_____
_____
_____
_____
_____
_____
_____
_____
_____
_____
_____
_____
_____
_____
_____

Prayer
*Lord, training up these children in the way they should go is an awesome
task and too big for me to attempt alone. Please come alongside me and
help me raise them according to Your ways. May they cling to You and never
depart from the truths that will bring them the abundant life and promise
You have in store for them.*

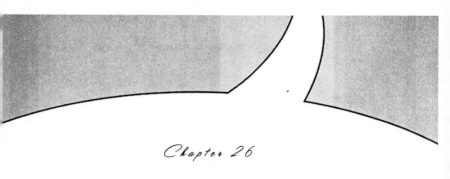

gifts with a card attached

· ·

> My son, if you accept my words and store up
> my commands within you, turning your ear to
> wisdom and applying your heart to understanding,
> and if you call out for insight and cry aloud for
> understanding, and if you look for it as for silver
> and search for it as for hidden treasure, then
> you will understand the fear of the LORD
> and find the knowledge of God.
>
> Proverbs 2:1–5 NIV

Steve and I had already chosen and purchased the presents we were going to give Tucker for his thirteenth birthday, but I wanted to give them more meaning. So, I looked over each of the gifts and asked the Lord to show me how they might represent more than just fun things I wanted to give to my son. I ended up writing a series of notes that went along with each present to commemorate this important, coming-of-age event. I wrote:

Happy Thirteenth Birthday, Tucker!

Guitar kit: It's time for you to work on building your relationship with your dad. As you spend time together building this guitar, you can watch and learn how to become a man of God.

Contact lenses: With this gift comes the privilege of staying up until ten o'clock. I will still put you to bed at nine, but you may stay up for an extra hour and read. It is also a good time to continue the habit of reading one chapter in your Bible every day.

Shower CD player: From today on, we will help you make decisions about media choices, rather than making them for you. When it comes to music, movies, and video games, we will listen to you, research together, and help you listen to the Holy Spirit for guidance about the influences you allow into your heart.

Chocolate cigar: You probably won't have to deal with friends trying to get you to smoke cigars, but the people you surround yourself with over the next few years will become more and more critical to the way your life turns out. With each new relationship ask yourself, *Will this friend draw me away from the things of the Lord or stand with me to make good choices?*

Family birthday cards: Other than Jesus, there is no more important relationship in life than the one with your family. Value it as your greatest treasure. Polish it as silver, and it will last as long as gold.

Magic Mountain tickets: Fun is very important, especially given the way God made you. This is a good thing. With the wonderful sense of humor that God gave you, however, you will need to make sure you don't put the goal of having fun above other people, your reputation, or God's idea of fun. We trust you to have a good, fun time with a friend at Magic Mountain.

Your own phone: Words bring life or death. God has anointed your tongue, and Satan knows it. Be careful to weigh each word that comes out of your mouth. Ask yourself ... does it make God smile?

Six dollars (to rent a game): Part of becoming an adult is learning how to handle money. There is no greater advice than to always tithe to God first. He will supply your every need—and most of your wants.

Trip to San Francisco with Dad: From today forward, we will listen to your requests and desires more. We want to be able to communicate openly with you about anything and everything. We are not only your parents but also your best friends, and we always will be. Not if you fail, but when you fail; not if you sin, but when you sin. You can trust us, and I know we can trust you.

. . . .

Speaking
mom-ese

Write down some of the abstract
concepts you have been trying to
teach your children, such as wisdom, respect, honesty, and humility.
Now ask the Lord to help you think
of ways you can impress these important values upon their hearts. _____

_____

_____

_____

_____

_____

_____

_____

_____

_____

_____

_____

_____

_____

_____

_____

_____

_____

_____

_____

Prayer

*Lord, help me to be creative in teaching and training my children. Give me
illustrations, object lessons, and stories that will stay in their hearts long
after my words have flown out of their heads.*

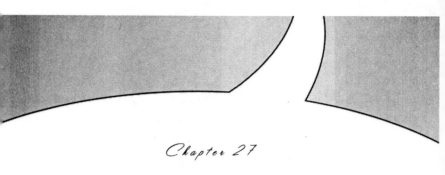

Chapter 27

calling all intercessors!

. . . .

**So we have continued praying for you ever since
we first heard about you. We ask God to give you a
complete understanding of what he wants to do in
your lives, and we ask him to make you wise with
spiritual wisdom.**

Colossians 1:9 NLT

I remember our very first MomTime Get-A-Way at the
Opryland Hotel in Nashville. Oh my goodness, it was so exciting!
The weekend confirmed my belief that women everywhere are
desperate for some stress-relieving laughter, get-real girl talk,
whispers from the Lord, and a few prizes thrown in for good
measure.

As confident as I felt that these fun weekend retreats for
moms were in line with God's heart, I still had moments of sheer
terror. The scope of what we were attempting was enormous. I
like to come up with grand ideas. My manager, Ron Smith, is

good at believing they can happen, and my beloved husband, Steve, is a master of the details. But if God doesn't bless our plans, then they are a waste of time, not to mention money!

Fortunately, we didn't have to rely on our own strength; we had hundreds of people praying for us and for the event. And God heard their prayers.

I believe strongly in the power of intercessory prayer, I understand my desperate need for it, and I'm not too proud to ask for it. (So please pray for me.) To be honest, I'm not terribly good at it myself, though. Sure, I pray every morning and throughout the day, but I'm not what you would call a prayer warrior. Don't get me wrong. I know that God has called all of us to pray, but I believe there are some people God has blessed with the calling and a greater ability to intercede on behalf of others. These intercessors find praying to be as natural as breathing. They spend hours praying for people they don't even know. If you are an intercessor, God has blessed you with a magnificent gift—one that has the power to shape eternity. And the best way to say thanks to the giver of that gift is, quite simply, to use it.

The Apostle Paul exhorted Timothy not to "neglect the gift" he had been given but to practice and devote himself to it (see 1 Timothy 4:13—15). Do you believe that your prayers *really* make a difference? Are you willing to invest the time, heart, and energy to become a real prayer warrior? Are you one of those godly women who stand ready and willing to prayerfully bear the burdens of others? If so, please don't minimize the value of that gift. Believe me, prayer doesn't come easily to everyone. You are special, and the body of Christ—in fact, the whole world— desperately needs you.

Whatever strength God has blessed you with, whether it is prayer or hospitality or teaching or mercy, take it seriously. When you use your gifts to honor God, you will be making an eternal difference in the lives of others.

. . . .

Speaking mom-ese

If you know God has called you to a ministry of prayer, list some extravagant prayer requests and ask God to give you the faith to believe He can make them happen. If, like me, you aren't what you would call a prayer warrior, make a list of things you need prayer for and then don't be ashamed to ask someone to pray with you about them. _____

_____

_____

_____

_____

_____

_____

_____

_____

_____

_____

_____

_____

_____

_____

Prayer

Dear Lord, thank You for the power of prayer. I don't know why You chose to give Your children the ability to change lives through our simple words to You, but I'm grateful You did. Help me not to take this responsibility for granted. Make me someone devoted to prayer—someone who is making an eternal difference in the world.

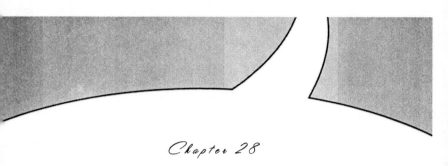

Chapter 28

it's a God thing

· ·

**"Can you solve the mysteries of God?
Can you discover everything there is to know
about the Almighty? Such knowledge is higher than
the heavens—but who are you? It is deeper than the
underworld—what can you know in comparison to
him? It is broader than the earth and wider
than the sea."**

Job 11:7–9 NLT

$\mathcal{I}$t's easy for us to wonder if God even notices what's going on in our lives. Surely, we think, He has more important things on His mind than our little problems! Why would God hear our prayers and move the mountains in our midst? They must look like anthills from His perspective. Why would He bother?

To our human minds, that line of reasoning makes sense— but God's character is so much greater than that. We may not be able to fathom how He could be intimately aware of our every thought and concern, but He is (see Psalm 139). The Lord cares deeply about the things we care about.

I was reminded of God's awesome love for His children at a retreat I hosted in Houston. During one session, the most amazing God-thing happened. To get everyone acquainted, I asked the ladies to introduce themselves and say how many children they had. At one table there was a mom who had come to the retreat alone. She introduced herself to the group at her table and said, "My name is Cindy*, and I have a daughter here on earth and another one in heaven." One of the moms at the table said, "My friend, Laura*, here, also lost a daughter." The two moms felt an instant bond.

A few minutes later, Cindy looked at Laura's nametag and noticed her last name was Yankowitz*. "Yankowitz?" she mused out loud. "Melissa Rose Yankowitz*?"

Laura heard her and was astonished. "How do you know my daughter's name?"

Cindy replied, "Because my little girl is buried two tombstones down from your little girl. For eight years, I've visited my daughter's grave and noticed the dates on your daughter's tombstone. I've often thought of the mother who also lost a child so young."

These two moms came from different areas of Texas and had never met. God brought one of them to the mothers' meeting

(*These names have been changed.)

alone, and He sat them down at the very same table on the first night of the retreat. Was this meeting a mere coincidence? Don't believe that for a second! God wanted these two women to meet, and He led them to a place where they could do so.

Just as God had plans for those two women, He also has plans for you and your family. You may not realize it, but God is always leading you somewhere. Your job, of course, is to follow Him—even if you don't understand precisely where you're going or why.

The next time you can't feel God's presence and you wonder if He's too far away to notice little ol' you, remember Cindy and Laura's story. The Lord is always at work in the lives of His children. He never falls asleep on the job. Sometimes His hand is more noticeable than at other times, but even when it isn't obvious to you, He is busy doing things you can't even imagine. If you surrender your hopes and fears to God and simply trust Him, He will move heaven and earth—and even a few anthills—to accomplish His will in your life.

. . . .

Speaking
mom-ese

When you begin to doubt His role in your life, remember that if God can move mountains, He can also make divine appointments for you. Write down a few examples of times in your life in which God orchestrated incredible events. _____

_____

_____

_____

_____

_____

_____

_____

_____

_____

_____

_____

_____

_____

_____

_____

_____

_____

Prayer
Lord, I completely surrender to Your will for my life. Do whatever it takes to accomplish Your will in and through me, and continue to lead me to Your divine appointments. Thank You for being interested in the tiniest details of my life.

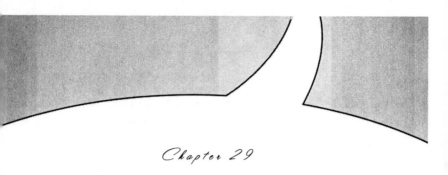

Chapter 29

where is God in all of this?

- -

**Look, he is coming with the clouds, and every eye
will see him.**

Revelation 1:7a NIV

I felt for a long time that the Lord was rearranging various pieces of my life to create a picture that I would eventually
call "MomTime Get-A-Ways." So Steve and I followed God's
prodding and began planning these events. Our first Get-A-
Way was at the Opryland Hotel in Nashville. As I walked down
the hallway of the hotel to the ballroom to begin the very first
Get-A-Way, I prayed silently, *Lord, I've done everything I can to
prepare for this weekend. Please anoint my efforts and take over
from here.* In that hallway, He spoke to my heart and confirmed
our plans. *Lisa,* I felt Him say, *I've prepared you your whole life for
this moment.* It was true. Every piece of the MomTime weekend

retreats had been birthed at different times of my life. Now, each one of those life experiences had come together to create this "baby."

The first Get-A-Way was successful in almost every way. As I remarked to Steve, "God showed up!" We lost tons of money on it, but we understood that was to be expected in any new endeavor. The Lord had provided for us the previous year through many speaking engagements, and we were able to take the financial hit without going into debt. Steve and I believed the Lord had confirmed to us multiple times that He was blessing our efforts, so we hired a woman part-time and scheduled a second event in Atlanta for the following spring. After doing the math, we determined we would need 350 ladies to show up at each event to break even. We had 250 in Nashville and just under 200 in Atlanta.

Despite the small numbers, we scheduled two more Get-A-Ways the next fall: one in Houston and another in Nashville. We had a fabulous weekend in Nashville with about two hundred moms. The Houston weekend was terrific, too, but it brought in just one hundred women. By this time, we were growing concerned about whether we had truly heard from the Lord. We had to take out a loan against our home in order to cover the losses.

After much soul searching and grieving, Steve and I decided that rather than continue to push the events, we would let our dream die if that's what God had in mind. It was a tough decision, and I still haven't come up with any answers about why our

MomTime Get-A-Ways didn't turn out the way we anticipated. On a much smaller scale, it felt similar to that of a mother giving birth to a stillborn child. The idea was conceived as a gift from God. I nurtured it for months, being careful to provide every resource possible to ensure the greatest chance of health. But despite bringing it to full term, laboring with it, and experiencing the pain and stretching of making it a reality, the dream died.

Are you in the midst of circumstances that don't make sense? Do you find yourself asking, "Where is God in all of this?" I've asked the same question. I don't believe there is any shame in wanting answers to a painful situation. I also don't believe that God is insulted when we question Him. I'm learning, though, that I must be content if God doesn't answer ... at least not right away.

During those times, I find comfort in one of my favorite devotions from Oswald Chambers. If you are experiencing pain, my prayer is that it will give you some peace, too:

Behold, He cometh with clouds. —Revelation 1:7 KJV[1]

In the Bible clouds are always connected with God. Clouds are those sorrows or sufferings or providences, within or without our personal lives, which seem to dispute the rule of God. It is by those very clouds that the Spirit of God is teaching us how to walk by faith.

It is possible to ask questions of God without questioning God.

. . . .

Write down some of the questions you would like to ask God. It's okay to be honest with Him about your frustrations, disappointments, and questions. What's most important is that you communicate your feelings to Him. _____

_____
_____
_____
_____
_____
_____
_____
_____
_____
_____
_____
_____
_____
_____
_____
_____
_____
_____
_____

Prayer

*Lord, some things just don't make sense. To be honest, I admit that
sometimes I don't agree with how You have allowed things to turn out.
But I will trust You, even when I can't see You or understand Your ways.
I know that You are here and that You are good.*

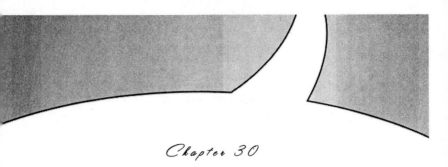

Chapter 30

taking the land

. . . .

**The LORD says, "I will guide you along the best
pathway for your life. I will advise you and watch
over you."**

Psalm 32:8 NLT

I was definitely excited, but despite my initial eagerness to
uproot, I suddenly felt hesitant after Steve made the final decision for us to move to Texas. Maybe it was because I'd wanted
to make the move so badly that I had spent months in prayer,
trying to let go of my own agenda so that I could be ready and
willing to follow God's plan for our family. Or it could have been
because I didn't expect to hear from God until the spring.

So much for my spiritual hunches. My confirmation came on
New Year's Day. I was doing a Beth Moore Bible study, and that
day the passage covered the story of Joshua and Caleb, the only

two guys with enough guts and faith to scout out the Promised Land. In that devotion, Beth asks:

> Are you standing at your own Kadesh-barnea? Have you found yourself on the brink of the place for which God has long been preparing you? A location? A place of service? A circumstance? A position? Something for which you sense He has been preparing you for a long time? Now that you see Him fulfilling His promise to use you and have gone through excruciating preparation toward that end, are you filled with fear? An overwhelming feeling of unreadiness? A sudden emotion that this may not be what you wanted? A little sorry you volunteered to go wherever and do whatever?

The ending verse, Joshua 1:9, hit me square in my heart: "Have I not commanded you? Be strong and of good courage; do not be afraid, nor be dismayed, for the Lord your God is with you wherever you go" (NKJV). The last words for the day were, "Take the land, beloved." Those words gave me the confidence that I needed.

I can't tell you how grateful I was that the Lord spoke directly to me from His Word, confirming that He wanted us in Texas. I trust my husband and his anointing as the head of our home, but I still needed that assurance from my Father in heaven.

Sometimes, God prepares a path that will take us to a place of great potential, a promised land or a place of service for which He has been carefully preparing us. It may be a promise we've been waiting for Him to fulfill. Even so, we might find ourselves suddenly frightened or doubtful. When that happens, our challenge is to be "strong and of good courage," and in Beth's words to "take the land, beloved."

. . . .

Speaking
mom-ese

Describe a place, service, responsibility, or challenge you believe God has led you toward. Then prayerfully ask Him to continue leading you along the path of His choosing. _____

_____
_____
_____
_____
_____
_____
_____
_____
_____
_____
_____
_____
_____
_____
_____
_____
_____
_____
_____
_____
_____

Prayer

Lord, give me the courage to take hold of the promises You fulfill in my life.
Help me to hear Your words of confirmation, and then give me the faith to
act on those directives. Thank You for preparing good things for me.

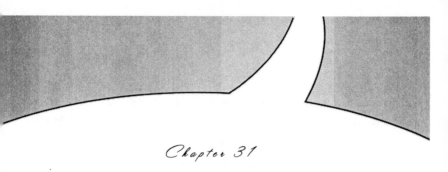

the sacrifice of praise

. . . .

**Through Him then, let us continually offer up a
sacrifice of praise to God, that is, the fruit of lips
that give thanks to His name.**

Hebrews 13:15 NASB

I remember the day of the setback, when the deal fell through
on the sale of our California house. I hated the thought of putting the house back on the market, keeping it all neat and tidy,
having people traipse through it, possibly having to pay a real-
tor fee, possibly needing to take a contingency offer this time, or
lowering the sales price. I could have worried, "What if we don't
sell it in time?" But instead of fretting, I tried to look at this
problem as an opportunity to show the Lord how much I trusted
in Him and His sovereignty.

I received the call from the ex-buyer while I was in the middle of singing along to a worship CD. After a very difficult conversation, I returned to the point in the CD where I had left off. The next three songs resonated with me and encouraged me to praise God for who He is, not for what He does.

The first song was "Blessed Be the Lord God Almighty." The song describes God's unchanging character with the line "who was, and is, and is to come." Through those lyrics, I was reminded of the verse in Hebrews 13:8, which says that Jesus is the same yesterday (when we had an awesome deal), today (when it fell through), and forever (when we will see His ultimate plans).

The next song was "Come, Now Is the Time to Worship." The main message of this song is that when Jesus returns, everyone will bow down and worship Him—but that those who worship Him now, before they see Him return in all His glory, will be blessed. I realized that it was easy to worship God when I could see how He had planned to sell our house and provide for us. But the true blessing would come now, when I chose to worship Him on faith, without knowing how everything was going to turn out.

The third song was "Take My Life," which describes the writer's desire to be thankful in all things. Usually, when I sang it, I concentrated on all the blessings the Lord had bestowed on me. But that day, I realized I also needed to make sure that I was thanking Him just for who He is.

Each of the tracts on the CD, in its own way, helped me to

better understand a line in another praise song, which says, "We bring the sacrifice of praise into the house of the Lord." Sometimes we must concentrate on praising God even when we don't feel like it, even when we can't see Him working. Otherwise, it is easy to start focusing on the *blessing* rather than the *Blesser*.

· ·

Speaking
m o m - e s e

Write a letter of thanks to God—not for what He has done, but for who He is.

_____

_____

_____

_____

_____

_____

_____

_____

_____

_____

_____

_____

_____

_____

_____

Prayer
Lord, You are the same yesterday, today, and forever (see Hebrews 13:8).
Thank You that Your character never changes. Help me to confidently praise
You no matter what the circumstances. I choose to worship You, Lord, and
trust Your holy name.

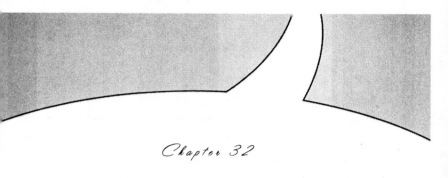

honesty pays

· ·

The godly are directed by their honesty.

Proverbs 11:5a NLT

We were building our house in Texas, and it had not been a good week. Our primary contact with the builder, the woman who sold us our house, was fired. Then the builder shut down work on the house for two days because of paperwork disputes. It looked like things wouldn't be ready until the middle of September, and that meant we would lose the interest rate we had locked in.

Exasperated, we finally got the company bigwigs to agree to a meeting. In our family's corner, Steve and I called in *our* biggest wig: my mother. For three hours, we hammered through each of the issues. Our primary concern was that many of the things the builder had verbally promised us were never officially written up in our contract. We also contended that it was unfair to expect us to pay for remedying mistakes the builders had made. On the other hand, the builders were worried because they thought we might not pay for some things that were ordered, since they didn't have it in writing.

I think I shocked one of the guys when I showed him an error that would have saved our family two thousand dollars. The man looked at me and asked, "Why did you point that out?"

"Because those are the kind of people you are dealing with," my mother responded. "You don't need to be worrying."

As we wrapped up the meeting, one of the gentlemen looked at me quizzically and said, "Thank you for your honesty."

I didn't realize how important that meeting was until we walked back over to the house. During our three-hour meeting, all heaven had broken loose. Where for the past few weeks, there had been two, maybe three trucks out front, now there were ten to twelve. The builders had called in other workers to quickly finish up the job! Suddenly, it was like a barn raising at our soon-to-be new house.

Our story about homebuilding and verbal contracts demonstrates a truth that all of us have been taught from childhood: honesty pays. Sometimes being honest is difficult. Sometimes being honest is painful. But God commands us to be honest all the time. In the book of Exodus, God did not say, "Thou shalt not bear false witness when it is convenient." God said, "Thou shalt not bear false witness" (Exodus 20:16 KJV). Period.

As children, we are taught that honesty is the best policy, but there's more to it than that. Honesty is not just the best policy—it is also *God's* policy. If we want to experience God's blessings, we must always speak the truth, despite the cost.

. . . .

Speaking
mom-ese

I once saw a sign that read, "Half truths are whole lies." Have you been tempted lately to tell "little white lies?" Have you rationalized any of your deceitful words or actions? Bring those areas to God and ask for Him to forgive your indiscretions. _____

_____
_____
_____
_____
_____
_____
_____
_____
_____
_____
_____
_____
_____
_____
_____
_____
_____
_____

Prayer

*"Test me, O LORD, and try me, examine my heart and my mind; for your love
is ever before me, and I walk continually in your truth"*
(Psalm 26:2–3 NIV).

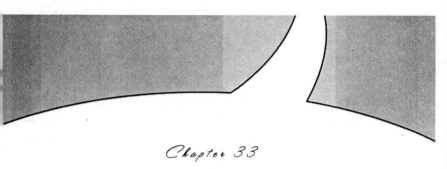

Chapter 33

break the selfishness
in me, Lord

. . . .

**Be devoted to one another in brotherly love.
Honor one another above yourselves.**

—Romans 12:10 NIV

"Mom," Tucker's voice boomed into my cell phone, "Dad broke
his arm. You'd better come quick."

I didn't believe my joke-a-minute son. Three years before, I
had been scrapbooking at the very same place when Steve had
fallen off the roof and broken his leg and both arms. "Put your
dad on the phone," I said warily.

When Steve got on the line, however, I could tell he was in
severe pain. So I hopped in the car and rushed home. When I
arrived, I found not only my husband but also Clancy holding
her arm and crying. Earlier that afternoon, Clancy had been

practicing handsprings when she landed the wrong way on her arm. She let out the kind of scream that indicates to every parent that something bigger is going on than childhood dramatics. When Steve ran outside to check on her, he tripped out the back door, slipped on a scooter, and broke his wrist.

Unfortunately, Steve hadn't broken just any wrist—he'd snapped his dominant one, the right wrist, and would be in a cast for six weeks. The timing was *terrible*. We were preparing to move, and in three weeks we needed to be completely packed and out of our house. *The things some people will do to get out of packing!* I thought, only half joking. Now, not only was I solely responsible for sorting through and packing our belongings, but I also had to tie my husband's shoes, sign his name, button his pants, apply his deodorant, and even wipe his … chin.

It wouldn't have been so bad except that Steve has very high standards for everything. That meant I couldn't just write something down for him. I had to write it in a certain spot, with "just-so" penmanship. I couldn't just sort through our stuff while he "oversaw" things. I had to pick up the very box he was looking at, find the very object he was pointing to with his left hand, and place the boxed object in the very place he wanted. And I couldn't just taxi him around. I had to drive in the very lane he thought I should be in. Believe me, if I'd ever had any doubts about the importance of submitting to my husband as the leader in our marriage, I wouldn't after this reprise of "headship."

The first few days were the toughest. Steve was irritable and in pain, and I was beyond annoyed. But when I realized the damage I was doing by acting impatient and inconvenienced to "punish" Steve for something he couldn't control, I asked God to change my attitude. With God's help, I started looking at Steve's injury as an opportunity to serve my husband without reserve. I realized that I don't often get the occasion to give and serve to this degree, expecting nothing in return—and I didn't want to waste this chance to love my husband in so many practical ways. God would help with the packing somehow.

. . . .

Speaking
mom-ese

Make a list of ways you could bless
your husband by serving him. Try
to accomplish one act of kindness
toward him each day, expecting
nothing in return._____

_____
_____
_____
_____
_____
_____
_____
_____
_____
_____
_____
_____
_____
_____
_____
_____
_____
_____
_____

Prayer

*Purify my heart, Lord, and cleanse me of my selfish motives. Help me to give
to others in the same way You give to me: without expectation of receiving
anything back, whether praise or other blessings. You notice my selflessness,
and Your pleasure in me is reward enough.*

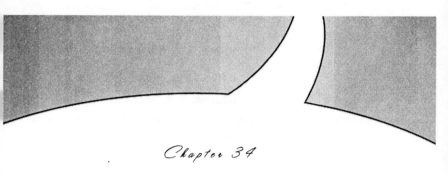

Chapter 34

rain, rain, go away

· ·

**This is the day the LORD has made.
We will rejoice and be glad in it.**

Psalm 118:24 NLT

One winter it seemed to rain like it did during the time of Noah and his ark. For days, it rained like cats and dogs. The weather was so bad, I'm sure I stepped in a "poodle"!

As a spoiled Southern Californian, I practically drown in even the lightest rain. Since I'd spent the majority of my life basking in the golden, balmy Los Angeles sunshine, I figured I had the freedom to whine about the weather. Not according to my mother! One morning at breakfast, as I was complaining about the stormy skies, she put me in my place.

"Oh, let me call the 'whaaaaaam-bulance.' Or perhaps

you should just order a 'whineburger and French cries,'" my mom said as she rolled her eyes. "Welcome to the real world, sister, where we have all kinds of weather."

As usual, Mom was right—in more ways than one. All of us must live through some rainy days, both literally and spiritually. Life's dark days give us the opportunity to grow in ways we may not otherwise have. But God does not force us to learn through challenges; we must embrace His lessons for ourselves. When the rain pours down by the bucketful, we're often tempted to whine, to complain, and to do little else. By giving in to negativity, though, we lose sight of our blessings. Ironically, most of us have more blessings than we can count, but we still find reasons to complain about the minor frustrations of everyday life, including the weather.

Are you easily irked by long lines, late people, carpet stains, and misplaced binkies? Are you tempted to whine about the inevitable challenges of life? Don't do it! Today and every day, make it a practice to count blessings, not raindrops. It's the godly way to live. Remember, the sun does eventually come out, and the ground dries up. In fact, in some places, it gets hot—so hot that the once soggy earth cracks and breaks open (something else I've been tempted to complain about!).

Rather than complain, try to simply appreciate each day for what it brings. With a lot of time, God's rain can perform incredible miracles, even changing the shape of a mountain. Ask God to give you the patience to endure a little rain. He just may be using it to mold you into His image.

· ·

Speaking mom-ese

Make a list of the things you usually complain about, and then vow to complain less and thank God more.

_____

_____

_____

_____

_____

_____

_____

_____

_____

_____

_____

_____

_____

_____

_____

_____

_____

_____

_____

_____

Prayer
*Lord, forgive me for complaining when life is not 70 degrees and balmy.
I want to praise You for the sun and the rain, knowing that You
are the Creator of both.*

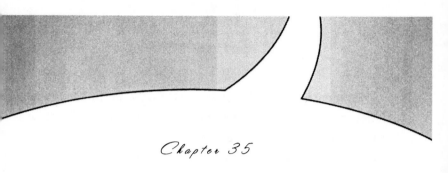

Chapter 35

thank God for take-out

· ·

**So then, just as you received Christ Jesus as Lord,
continue to live in him, rooted and built up in him,
strengthened in the faith as you were taught, and
overflowing with thankfulness.**

Colossians 2:6–7 NIV

For our first Thanksgiving in Texas, I wanted to impress my friends and family, so I decided to cook the entire dinner myself. I certainly made an impression, all right! I put the green bean casserole on the top rack and burned the corn flakes to a crisp; I forgot the whipped cream for the pumpkin pie; I microwaved the rolls so long, they could have been used for doorstops; the squash casserole was so creamy it could have been drunk with a straw; the orange carrots were a little too *al dente*; the smoked turkey was cold; and the stuffing ... well, that had to be thrown in the trash can.

Everyone was kind, but throughout the meal, I heard the following remarks. My friend from Nashville told me, "I just love coming to your house, Lisa, because you always make me feel so much better about myself." Steve said, "Babe, next time, let's cater." My dad joked, "This dish must be for those who left their teeth at home." Thankfully, Tucker put his arm around me and said, "Mom, I think everything looks delicious!"

Even with all the problems, the meal turned out fine. It was edible, and besides, the best part was sitting around the table after dinner, talking and drinking coffee. And I do make a mean cup of coffee!

That day, as I had cooked—and burned—the meal, I made a mental list of things I was thankful for. What I came up with isn't particularly deep, and if I were to do it again today, some of the items probably would not be at the top of my list. But here are my random thoughts of thankfulness from that first Thanksgiving in Texas:

I'm thankful that I live close to a Super Target store.

I'm thankful that I drive by a pasture with longhorns, a red barn, a pond, and a big tree on my way to the interstate.

I'm thankful that Clancy gives me no less than twenty-five kisses a day.

I'm thankful that Haven still sits in my lap.

I'm thankful that Tucker enjoys staying up late talking to me.

I'm thankful that I get to spend all day, everyday, with my husband—and I enjoy it.

I'm thankful that I've sinned greatly, because I know love and mercy.

I'm thankful for days with nothing to do.

I'm thankful for unlimited long distance so I can talk to my mother five times a day, no matter where my travels take me.

I'm thankful for my Nanny.

I'm thankful for mornings that begin with a hot cup of coffee and a Beth Moore Bible study.

I'm thankful for long plane rides with a good book.

I'm thankful for Sunday afternoon naps.

I'm thankful for the Internet.

I'm thankful for homeschooling.

I'm thankful that in heaven I'll have time to play golf, plant a garden, get up-to-date with my scrapbooks, bake, snow ski, read all the books I've bought, sew clothes for my kids, quilt with my mother, play dominoes with my grandmother, learn to play the piano, and spend time with all my friends.

I'm thankful for knowing how to rest in God.

I'm thankful for stimulating conversation.

I'm thankful for the way the day smells first thing in the morning.

I'm thankful that I know to Whom I should direct my grateful heart.

• •

Speaking
mom-ese

It doesn't matter what time of year it is—it's always the season for thanksgiving! Write down a few of your own random thoughts of thankfulness. Now thank God for His sweet mercies in your life. _____

_____

_____

_____

_____

_____

_____

_____

_____

_____

_____

_____

_____

_____

_____

Prayer

*I have so much to be thankful for, Lord. Let me never forget that every good
and perfect gift comes from You (see James 1:17).
Thank You for all that You do for me each day.*

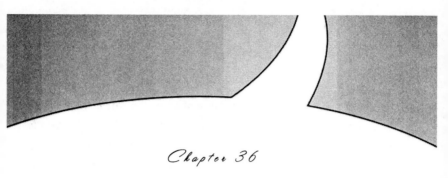

Chapter 36

the power of one

. . . .

**Let no one despise your youth, but be an example
to the believers in word, in conduct, in love,
in spirit, in faith, in purity.**

1 Timothy 4:12 NKJV

Isn't it incredible what a difference—what a life-altering difference—one person, obeying his or her calling, can make in this world? I like to call this phenomenon "the power of one." Take, for example, Mel Gibson, who overcame numerous obstacles to make the movie *The Passion of the Christ*. What a worldwide impact this one man, following the Lord's prompting, will have on eternity! (When we were discussing this, Clancy asked, "Does that mean Mel Gibson is a Christian?" I answered, "Apparently so." "Cool!" she responded. "I'd love to spend eternity with Mel Gibson!")

Mel Gibson is a great example of how God can work through one person. But what I find even more poignant are the people I know—the ordinary people around me—who are simply doing what the Lord has called them to do, without notice or fanfare. My children's youth pastor, Chris King, immediately comes to mind. This young man's fingerprints will leave an eternal mark on all three of my kids, but especially upon my son. I don't know exactly which direction Tucker's life will take, but I do believe that God has anointed Chris to help direct Tucker's course at a pivotal point in his life.

When we moved to Texas, one of the things we looked most forward to was getting involved in a small, neighborhood church. Because we homeschool, I knew the majority of relationships my kids made would come through our church. That's why the idea of a local church, located close to home, was so appealing to us. We visited many churches in our area and felt confident that we could worship and serve at any number of them.

God had other plans. In the middle of our search, our children were invited to Fellowship Church, which is twenty to twenty-five minutes from our house and serves seventeen thousand to nineteen thousand people between five weekend services. It wasn't exactly what we had in mind, but we figured it would be fun to visit.

What we didn't expect was the personal touch and tenacity of the youth department. Within days, Chris King called our house and talked to Steve, asking if he could drop by sometime to spend a little one on one time with the children, outside the wild-and-crazy atmosphere of youth group.

Less than five months later, we were regularly attending Fellowship Church. Sure, the pastor, Ed Young Jr., is a fascinating, uncompromising, and relevant preacher. Absolutely, the music rivals any professional Christian concert. But ultimately, we chose our church because of one young man and the time he took to welcome our three children.

We are grateful to Chris and Janice, Pace and Sarah, Andy and Mandy, and all the countless volunteers, youth workers, musicians, and small group leaders who make up a youth group that my kids can't wait to attend each week. Collectively, these servants are a gift from God. Individually, they are "the power of one."

. . . .

Speaking mom-ese

Think about some of the people God has placed in your life. What about new neighbors? Single moms? Children from broken homes? The elderly or lonely? Write down specific ways God can use you to make an eternal difference in their lives. _____

_____
_____
_____
_____
_____
_____
_____
_____
_____
_____
_____
_____
_____
_____
_____
_____
_____
_____
_____

Prayer

Lord, use me to touch someone's life in a significant way. I confess that I sometimes let busyness or fear keep me from reaching out to others. Please forgive me and change me so I can be used by You to make a difference.

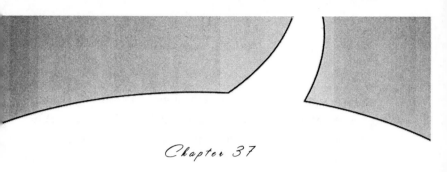

Chapter 37

achieving greatness

. . . .

But the greatest among you shall be your servant.

Matthew 23:11 NASB

$\mathcal{I}$'ve always looked up to my Uncle Jimmy. For as long as I can remember, he's been a faithful, steadfast man of God. He has a deep, abiding faith that is central to every decision he makes, but unless you observed him quietly for a long period of time, you wouldn't necessarily know it. His ministry is not *talking about* the Lord, it is *walking with* the Lord.

Every morning, Uncle Jimmy gets up before sunrise and spends an extended period of time praying for each member of his family. He impacts their lives with eternal significance, but for all intents and purposes, none of them know. He doesn't advertise this routine. Uncle Jimmy's prayer time is just a special ritual between a father and a Father.

Uncle Jimmy visited my Nanny each day after his morning coffee and prayers. He would fix her breakfast, take out her trash, mow her lawn, vacuum her floor, and do whatever else she needed help with. Then he would sit down and talk with her. (The sweetest gift!)

I believe acts of ministry like Uncle Jimmy's bring a bigger smile to the Lord's face than the weekends I speak before a thousand people, sell books, and bring home an honorarium. We are often tempted to believe that we need to become an author, a speaker, a preacher, or a missionary in order to serve God. The truth is, though, we can and should serve Him without ever leaving our neighborhood.

Instead of searching the world over to find some far-flung ministry, ask yourself this: how does God want me to serve others today? Not tomorrow. Not some day in the distant future. What needs to be done right here, right now?

Whatever your path, whatever your calling, wherever you happen to find yourself, serving others is an integral part of God's plan for you. And you can be sure that each day of your life—including today—God will give you opportunities to serve Him by serving others. Don't shirk those opportunities. They are God's gift to you! They are His way of allowing you to achieve greatness in His kingdom ... just like Uncle Jimmy.

• •

Speaking
m o m - e s e

Write down at least ten opportunities for you to serve others that won't require you to travel more than five miles from home. _____

_____

_____

_____

_____

_____

_____

_____

_____

_____

_____

_____

_____

_____

_____

_____

_____

_____

_____

_____

_____

_____

_____

Prayer

Open my eyes, Lord, and help me see the many opportunities I have to serve You. I don't want to deem anyone unworthy of my time. Remind me that, in order to achieve greatness in Your kingdom, I must lay down my life and make time for others.

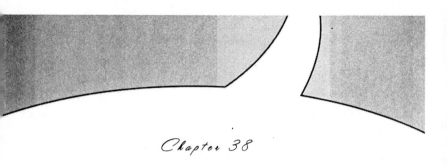

Chapter 38

a living epitaph

. . . .

**But the lovingkindness of the LORD is from
everlasting to everlasting on those who fear Him,
and His righteousness to children's children,
to those who keep His covenant, and who remember
His precepts to do them.**

Psalm 103:17–18 NASB

$\mathcal{I}$'ve always loved to put my thoughts in writing, especially when I want to communicate something important. Why? Letters can become permanent, living expressions of our love for others. Whether I'm making a list of significant lessons I want my children to remember, or I'm simply writing a "love note" to a friend or family member, I believe my words have much more impact on paper than if I simply said them in passing.

I wrote the following letter to my grandmother on her ninety-second birthday, shortly before she passed away.

Dear Nanny,

There are so many times throughout the day that I think of you. Whenever someone starts talking badly about somebody else, I think of you. I remember when I was a little girl, my mother said to me, "Nanny never says a negative thing about anyone." At the time I thought, WOW. THAT WOULD BE HARD TO DO. But you taught me that it's possible. When you hear others gossiping, you always make a point to say something kind about the other person.

This brings up another thing you've taught me: to "kill 'em with kindness." You are the best at this. You never overcome evil with evil, but always overcome evil with good. I have seen this time and time again in your life. You are a wise lady. It works!

I also think of you whenever I run into a fan. You wrote to half of them at one time or another when they were just kids. What an impact you made on their lives! They usually stopped writing fan letters to me and started calling and visiting you as their surrogate grandma. You've taught me to think of each fan meeting as an opportunity to touch someone's life, even if it is simply with a smile.

I remember as a Mouseketeer, I learned from you to always "wave at the security guard" on the way into the lot. You knew that no position was to be treated with more or less respect than another. Showing respect for authority was important, but showing respect for those in a position beneath your own was even more righteous.

Whenever I'm mad at Steve, I think of you. That may sound odd, but I watched you be a loving, respectful, submissive wife in harder times than I could imagine. If you could trust God enough in those kinds of situations, then I can surely forgive my husband for minor annoyances and faults.

There are three things, above all others, that I believe I learned (or inherited) from you: first, my love for being a mother. You have three godly children who adore you. That says so much about what kind of mother you are, especially since you raised them through childhood circumstances that could have turned any one of them in the wrong direction.

Second, your trust in the Lord. I remember a counselor once told me that the only explanation for why I had so much peace was that I must be living in denial. Well, we both know it isn't denial. But there isn't really an explanation that would make sense to this world. The truth is that I was just born with the deep knowledge that I could trust the Lord, no matter what the world threw my way. I notice that you live the same way, so God must have passed down that "trust" gene through you the same way He passed down your "Texas 42" gene to me.

This brings me to the times I think of you the most—when playing dominoes! I love being your partner. I appreciate you, the "Texas 42 queen," for being so sweet about playing with me. I know there have been many times I've made a boneheaded play and you just let it go. You are a ruthless, serious domino champion, but it really doesn't matter to you whether you win or lose—you just love to play. And so do I, especially cause I have the best partner who ever lived!

Thank you, Nanny, for giving me so many opportunities to think about you throughout the day. Thinking of you always makes me smile and offer a quick thanks to the Lord for allowing me the privilege of having you as my grandmother.

I lubba you, too,

Lisa

· ·

Speaking mom-ese

What do you want your children and grandchildren to remember about you? Write down those qualities and then ask the Lord to make them such a part of your character that they will leave a godly impact on future generations. _____

_____

_____

_____

_____

_____

_____

_____

_____

_____

_____

_____

_____

_____

_____

_____

_____

_____

_____

Prayer

Dear Father in heaven, let my light shine so that others will see my good works and give glory to You. Work Your character into my heart and life so that I may reflect Your glory to those around me—especially to my family.

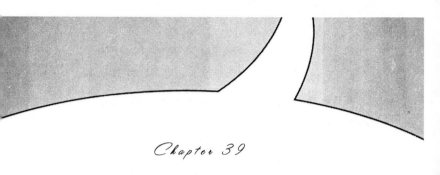

Chapter 39

the money game

· ·

**Thus all the tithe of the land, of the seed of
the land or of the fruit of the tree, is the Lord's;
it is holy to the Lord.**

Leviticus 27:30 NASB

Children grow up—fast! Once mine hit the teenage years, I felt in some ways like we were closer than ever and in other ways as if they were pulling away. I sensed an urgent responsibility to prepare them for life, but at the same time I could tell that my level of input was diminishing. With all those hormones, my kids were changing daily, and so, I realized, must my parenting.

For a long time, Steve and I chose not to give our children an allowance. We exchanged the word "chores" for "ways to serve the family." We provided avenues for them to make extra money, mostly through up-and-over jobs, and I occasionally paid them to read certain books.

When they become adolescents, though, they began wanting more and more things that I simply wasn't willing to spend my money on, such as shirts that cost more than I thought they were worth, CDs I couldn't understand, and "mall money." So Steve and I decided to adjust our previous philosophy and started paying them for showing responsibility in their "job" of growing up. We looked at each child individually and determined what he or she could earn in "big" money by doing extra jobs around the house, such as office or yard work. We also evaluated their areas of weakness and added an extra incentive payment if they improved in that area without having to be reminded. We even opened a checking account for each one of them—an event so exciting that it was worthy of a two-page scrapbook layout!

Right away, all three kids handled their money differently. Clancy began computing how long it would take her to save up for a car, asking Steve how much she would need to keep in mind for insurance. Tucker spent all of his money downloading songs from the Internet. And Haven's money burned a hole in her purse until she got to the mall to buy clothes.

Up to that point, whenever they had received gift money, the kids had given Steve and me 10 percent so we could add it to our online giving program. Once we decided to open checking accounts for them, though, we wanted to drive home the thrill of giving in a more personal way. So the first week we paid Tucker, Haven, and Clancy their grown-up money, we had them write their own tithe checks to drop in the offering bag during church.

The sweetest thing about this new development was the Lord's touch on the matter. Incredibly, that Sunday our pastor, Ed Young Jr., spoke about tithing. We had attended Fellowship Church for almost a year and had never heard the pastor talk about money. During the sermon, Pastor Young even admitted that out of the seven hundred or so sermons he'd preached at Fellowship Church, fewer than twenty of them had been about tithing and stewardship.

It was with great pride that I watched my children tithe with their own checks that first week. It wasn't just that they were taking responsibility; it also signified an important step in their walk toward spiritual maturity. I pray that the practice of tithing stays with our kids. Our family has been through many financial challenges, but no matter how tight things have gotten, we've always brought God the "first fruits" of our labors.

Through those lean times, God has taught me over and over that we can't out-give Him. When we trust Him and play by His rules, we always win. Even if we are behind at halftime, we will still win in the end, and often just in time to witness some miraculous provision that He gives on our behalf. I consider it a privilege to teach my children how to play the game of life God's way, because I know that He—even more than I—wants them to live the life abundant.

. . . .

Do you have a plan for teaching
your children to be good stewards
of their time, talents, and money?
What is your own philosophy of
stewardship? Note some practical
ways you can help your children live
out this important commandment. _____

_____

_____

_____

_____

_____

_____

_____

_____

_____

_____

_____

_____

_____

_____

_____

_____

_____

Prayer
Thank You, Father, that all I have belongs to You. Help me to be a joyful
giver as I faithfully bring my tithe to you each week. Show me practical
ways that I can teach my children the joy of giving.

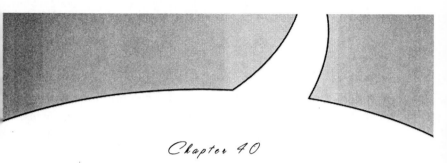

Chapter 40

the gospel according to mom

· ·

**Therefore you shall lay up these words of mine in
your heart and in your soul.... You shall teach them
to your children, speaking of them when you sit in
your house, when you walk by the way, when you
lie down, and when you rise up.**

Deuteronomy 11:18–19 NKJV

$\mathcal{I}$s anything more scary than watching our kids approach
the issue of recreational dating? Thankfully, most of the parents
Steve and I know agree that the whole idea of junior high
kids "going out" is silly—especially considering the fact that
we wouldn't actually allow our children to "go out" anywhere!
Even so, girls today are much more assertive than I remember,
and teenagers are extremely creative when it comes to dancing
around the rules.

I was especially concerned about Tucker, who was becoming
"friends" with certain girls who obviously had a lot more in mind.

To explain my apprehension to him, I asked him to read Proverbs chapter 7, which tells of a beautiful prostitute who leads a young man astray. As you can imagine, after Tucker read the Scripture, he said, "Mom! You are way overreacting. Are you calling my friends harlots? Don't worry so much. I'm fine!"

As a mom, I knew he might be fine today, but that if he didn't watch his steps, he might end up headed in the wrong direction tomorrow. So I wrote an interpretation of Proverbs 7 especially for Tucker.

Proverbs 7 or "The Gospel According to Mom"

My son, keep my words and if you value your life (v. 1).

Keep my commands. My law is the law—don't ever forget it (v. 2).

Tie a string around your finger or tattoo it on your heart (v. 3).

Say to wisdom, "You are my sister," and call understanding "Mom" (v. 4).

Listen to your "mom" and "sister," for they will keep you away from the girls (v. 5).

For from my minivan I looked through the window (v. 6).

And I saw a bunch of junior high boys

And one naïve young man in particular (v. 7).

Passing along the street near the mall,

And entering through Sears (v. 8),

Just after dark, before all the stores closed (v. 9).

And there a girl met him,

Wearing a shirt that revealed her belly button and her heart (v. 10).

She laughed way too loudly, and she was rarely at home with her parents (v. 11).

She seemed to turn up everywhere—at the mall, the movies,

And hanging out at friends' houses (v. 12).

She playfully hugged the young man and gave him a friendly kiss on the cheek.

With a spunky look she said to him (v. 13),

"I just came from youth group (v. 14).

"I was hoping to see you there, and when I didn't see you,

"I came looking for you. I'm so glad I found you (v. 15).

"I've fixed up my room really cool (v. 16).

"I bought a bunch of good smelling candles (v. 17).

"Why don't you come over and we can watch some movies (v. 18)?

"My parents aren't at home; they're away on a business trip (v. 19).

"They won't be back until Tuesday" (v. 20).

She looked so innocent that he bought it.

All she had to tell him was,

"I've never met a guy that I can talk to like you," and she had
  him (v. 21).

He fell for it, hook, line, and sinker (v. 22),

Until he felt the hook in his mouth.

Like a fish swimming for the worm,

He didn't know it was a trap until it was too late (v. 23).

Now listen up, kids, and listen up good (v. 24).

I know what I'm talking about:

Don't even look down that path (v. 25).

If you don't want to end up where that road is headed,

Then stay on the sidewalk.

Girls have been the fall of many strong Christian young men (v. 26).

They can lead you away from God, and you could end up losing
  your life—

At least the abundant one God has planned for you (v. 27).

Tucker is a wise young man, and he loves God, but he doesn't
yet have the discernment to see where certain paths might lead.
As his loving mother, I believe it is my God-given responsibility
to teach him what the Bible says about relationships—and to
make sure that he chooses his "friends" wisely.

· ·

Speaking mom-ese

What are your own relationship rules for your children? Even if your kids aren't old enough, these rules will come in handy sooner than you think. _____

_____

_____
_____
_____
_____
_____
_____
_____
_____
_____
_____
_____
_____
_____
_____
_____
_____
_____

Prayer

Lord, give me wisdom as I navigate the treacherous waters of raising children in today's world. Give my kids a healthy fear of You and a love for Your Word. May they hide that Word in their hearts so that they might not sin against You.

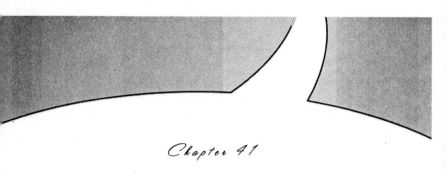

good thinking

. . . .

**Fix your thoughts on what is true and honorable
and right. Think about things that are pure and
lovely and admirable. Think about things that are
excellent and worthy of praise.**

Philippians 4:8b NLT

A friend of Tucker's had bought him a CD that was a compilation of secular songs. Granted, there was only one song he really wanted, but the rest of the CD was questionable. We told Tucker he would not be allowed to keep it.

"Mooom!" he complained. "You never let me listen to any 'good' music!" He tried to twist my arm, telling me that plenty of secular songs were acceptable. Why couldn't he listen to those, especially if they had good guitar solos? (Have I mentioned that Tucker lives and breathes the guitar?)

To explain my reasoning, I used the following illustration. "Tucker, imagine that there are two doors in front of you," I said.

"Behind one door is a room filled with snakes, scorpions, traps, poisons, and a handful of one-hundred-dollar bills. Behind the second door is a room filled with nothing but twenty-dollar bills. Which door should I encourage you to choose if you wanted to pick up some extra money?" The answer, of course, was door number two, which led to a room that contained both safety and abundance.

I told Tucker that like the room behind door number one, some secular CDs might contain a few *really* good guitar solos and some *really* good songs. But it wasn't worth wading through the snares of the enemy—poisonous images and lyrics that could come back to bite him. Ultimately, Tucker would be richer if he surrounded himself with music with which he could safely fill his mind and heart.

Of course, secular music isn't the only issue we've had to fight. From the time our kids were young, they have wanted to watch certain TV programs, go to certain movies, and read certain books and magazines that Steve and I found questionable as well. (For instance, I may have gone a bit overboard, but when they were little, I wouldn't even let my kids watch *The Little Mermaid* television cartoon because "Ariel" was often rebellious and disrespectful to her father.) Protecting them from these influences has been an ongoing battle. But I know there will come a day in the not-so-distant future when they will have to decide for themselves what door they are going to choose. Until then, I will continue to pray.

The enemy is working around the clock. In this fast-paced, technology-driven world, he is causing more pain and heartache than ever. Fortunately, when it comes to fighting Satan, we are never alone. God is always with us, and He gives us the strength to resist temptation whenever we ask. We need that strength—and so do our children.

· ·

Speaking mom-ese

What ungodly influences may be affecting your children? How can you best protect them and guide them on the right path? Make time to sit down and talk with your kids about your concerns. _____

_____

_____

_____

_____

_____

_____

_____

_____

_____

_____

_____

_____

_____

_____

_____

_____

_____

_____

Prayer

Lord, give my children a hunger for holiness. I pray that they will see Your Spirit as sweet and good, and the temptations of the world as the bitter fruit they are. Give us all the strength to live a life that is set apart for You.

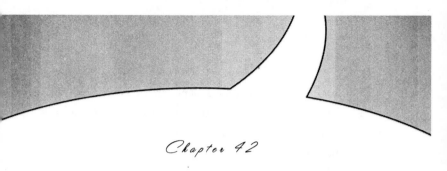

Chapter 42

who's responsible here?

...You must choose for yourselves today whom you
will serve.... As for me and my family,
we will serve the Lord.

Joshua 24:15 NCV

*W*ouldn't life be so much easier if we always said yes to our children? After all, a big part of being a mom is answering that never-ending string of queries, solicitations, and "I'm-down-on-my-knees-and-I'm-begging-you-Mom" requests that we all hear from time to time.

On second thought, maybe it would be easier if we always said no to our children. Then, we wouldn't have to think and pray about their requests, consider the circumstances, or evaluate the consequences. We could simply force our opinions and wisdom upon them, tell them what to do and what not to do, and refuse to hear their arguments. After all, parents do know best, right?

Unfortunately, being a mom is not that easy. We are not only responsible for our children, but we're also responsible to *teach* them responsibility—and sometimes we have to risk being irresponsible to do that.

Let me explain that last sentence by sharing a story. One Sunday morning, my daughter Clancy met a girl who happened to be wearing "the most fabulous" skirt Clancy had ever seen. The little girl told Clancy that the skirt came from abercrombie, a new "G-rated" Abercrombie & Fitch store designed for younger kids. Abercrombie & Fitch is a clothing store that uses insidious advertising to entice young customers. On my first visit to one of these stores, I saw a video loop showing a young man and woman removing all of their apparel. At that moment, I decided that our family, like many other Christian families, wouldn't buy—or wear—clothes from that store.

It took all Clancy's persuasive skills (which are considerable) to convince me to check out the "kid-friendly" version of Abercrombie & Fitch. Finally, I agreed. The new store, abercrombie, was definitely more acceptable, but I explained to Clancy that I simply could not, in good conscience, give my money to this company, whether they spelled their name with a big A or a little one. There was no guarantee that my thirty dollars wouldn't be used to fund the company's obvious agenda to do away with all the moral boundaries God has set up to protect young people.

Clancy was crushed; she desperately wanted the skirt. "Nobody has to know it came from this store," she pleaded. "It doesn't say the name anywhere on it."

That's when I realized that Clancy needed to make the decision about the skirt herself. So I told her she could stay in the store and think things over for a few minutes. Then, if she wanted to spend her own money to buy it, she was free to do so.

I waited outside, wondering what she would do. About five minutes later, Clancy came out of the store in tears. "I want you to know," she told me between sniffles, "that I don't agree with you. I didn't see anything wrong in that store, and that was the cutest skirt I've ever seen. *And you just don't understand!* But I can't disobey you because I can't stand the thought of your being disappointed in me, and I know I should trust your judgment, even if I don't want to . . . and I don't want to, but I will!"

I put my arm around Clancy and told her that I was proud of her, not only because I thought she made the right decision, but also because she was willing to trust my judgment. Of course, until Clancy walked out of that store empty-handed, I didn't know which choice she would make. But I did know that if she had decided to buy the skirt, that wouldn't have been the end of it. God, her heavenly Parent, would have continued the conversation.

Sometimes, being a mom means drawing a line and being willing and able to enforce the boundaries. And sometimes, it means drawing a line and then trusting our children with those boundaries. I don't know which is more difficult. What comforts me, though, is God's role in it all. In fact, one of my favorite Scriptures says, "All your children shall be taught by the LORD, and great shall be the peace of your children" (Isaiah 54:13 NKJV). I will never shirk my responsibility as a mother, but sometimes that means entrusting my responsibility to God.

. . . .

Speaking
mom-ese

Reflect on what it means to have your children be "taught by God." How can you, practically speaking, learn to trust God with your kids? Write a short prayer of consecration, asking the Lord to help you know when to step in and when to step back and let Him take control. _____

_____

_____

_____

_____

_____

_____

_____

_____

_____

Prayer

Heavenly Father, please write your laws upon my children's hearts and minds so that they may know Your ways and walk in them. Give me the wisdom to know when I should lead them, when I should walk beside them, and when I should hang back and trust them to follow You.

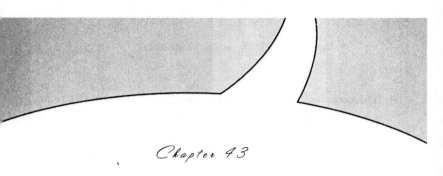

happy birthday, little lady

. . . .

**Train up a child in the way he should go: and when
he is old, he will not depart from it.**

Proverbs 22:6 KJV

*W*hen my oldest daughter, Haven, turned thirteen, we spent a day together at the spa. With each gift I gave her, I wrote a corresponding Scripture and a nugget of motherly advice. I've included a sampling of them to share with you.

Special Day with Mom—*When I was a child, I talked like a child, I thought like a child, I reasoned like a child. When I became a man [or a woman, in Haven's case!], I put childish ways behind me. —I Corinthians 13:11 NIV*

Sweetie, you are no longer a little girl, but a young woman.

Thirteen isn't just another birthday; it's a transition to another season of life. On this pivotal day, I want to tell you that you have successfully completed your little girl years! So far, you have been "in school" and I have been your teacher. Hopefully, the most important thing I have taught you is how to follow the Lord and obey His word. You are an awesome student. You have learned and obeyed, and I have full confidence that as you leave these little girl years, you will live out what you have learned.

Facial—*For if you just listen and don't obey, it is like looking at your face in a mirror but doing nothing to improve your appearance. You see yourself, walk away, and forget what you look like. But if you keep looking steadily into God's perfect law—the law that sets you free—and if you do what it says and don't forget what you heard, then God will bless you for doing it.* —*James 1:23–25* NLT

The word "hypocrite" was originally used to describe actors who wore masks. Now is the time for you to choose whether or not you are going to put on that mask: will you authentically "walk the talk" or will you simply play the part you have been taught since childhood? You have listened to me a lot. From this day forward, as you enter adulthood, you have the choice to either walk away from all you've learned or dig deeper into God's Word, obey Him, and discover His blessings for your life.

Pedicure—*If I then, the Lord and the Teacher, washed your feet, you also ought to wash one another's feet.*
—*John 13:14 NASB*

Sweetie, look for ways to serve others. Many people will look up to you because of your strong personality and confidence. That gives you an incredible opportunity to reflect Jesus by choosing to reach out to help other people. It's easy to think that the best way to serve God is to "do things for the Lord" through various ministry opportunities. Don't get me wrong—we can, and should, serve God in that way. But true acts of service, those times when we reach down to help others, often take more work than seemingly harder ministry jobs. Remember God tells us that we serve Him best when humble ourselves and serve others.

Skirt and shirt—*And I want women to be modest in their appearance. They should wear decent and appropriate clothing and not draw attention to themselves…. For women who claim to be devoted to God should make themselves attractive by the good things they do. —1 Timothy 2:9–10 NLT*

This one is going to be tough. You could wear a potato sack and still attract attention. But, dressing modestly can't be about skirt lengths and the width of shoulder straps. You simply need to ask yourself, "Could my clothing cause a young man's eyes to linger on my body and make him stumble?" Aim to please God and attract His attention by the good things you do. Then you will truly be beautiful.

Mother/daughter picture frame—*I prayed for this child, and the LORD has granted me what I asked of him.*
—1 Samuel 1:27 NIV

I wanted a daughter for as long as I could remember because I wanted to have the same kind of relationship with her that I have with my mother. Haven, we are so much alike. So far that is a good thing. I appreciate your strengths and understand your weaknesses. I'm so glad we are best friends. I don't take that for granted. I love you, my beautiful teenage daughter.

. . . .

Speaking mom-ese

Collect a few Scriptures that you would like to share with your children. Write them down and then add your own motherly advice. _____

_____
_____
_____
_____
_____
_____
_____
_____
_____
_____
_____
_____
_____
_____
_____
_____
_____
_____
_____

Prayer

Lord, keep my children's ears open to my motherly advice and Your Fatherly wisdom. May they close their ears to the teaching that suits their own opinions and desires. Instead, I pray that they would welcome Your truth and nothing but Your truth. (So help them, God!)

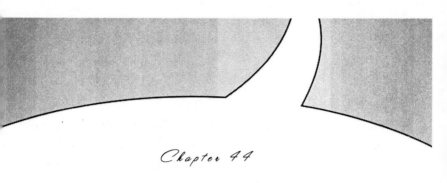

Chapter 44

parenting from the inside out

· ·

Don't fret or worry. Instead of worrying, pray. Let petitions and praises shape your worries into prayers, letting God know your concerns. Before you know it, a sense of God's wholeness, every- thing coming together for good, will come and settle you down. It's wonderful what happens when Christ displaces worry at the center of your life.

Philippians 4:6–7 MSG

Some days I wonder if there's anything tougher than raising teenagers! Well, maybe sending a man to the moon was a little more difficult than guiding youngsters toward adulthood, but since I wasn't part of the Apollo missions, I can't say for sure. What I can say is this: it isn't easy being the mom of active, growing adolescents.

To be honest with you, I felt like I was a pretty good parent as long as I was bigger than my kids—and I'm only half joking. As they've gotten older and older, though, things have changed . . . and being a good mom has gotten harder and harder. Like most moms, I felt much safer when I believed (rightly or wrongly) that I had more control over my children's lives. I've found that the faster my kids grow up, the harder it is for me to convince myself that I can truly "direct" their lives.

I, like you, firmly believe that I know what's best for my children. I want to help my kids avoid unnecessary pain (which, of course, I firmly believe they can do if they listen to my advice and obey my instructions!). But, part of parenting teenagers is letting them grow up and make independent decisions—even if those choices are wrong. It's terrifying knowing there is no guarantee that my children will choose to follow Jesus and His ways. So, I've learned to redirect my parenting passion. Now, when I'm tempted to lecture my children, I try to pray for them instead.

The power of prayer. These words are so familiar that sometimes we forget what they mean. Prayer is a powerful tool that allows us to communicate with the living God! It is not something to be taken lightly or to be used occasionally. After all, I can only do so much parenting from the outside in. Our heavenly Father does *His* work from the inside out. It's heartening to see Him work in my kids' lives, and I'm so thankful I can help. Every day I do my part by talking to my Creator about my kids.

Is prayer an integral part of your parenting plan, or is it a hit-or-miss habit? Make no mistake: the quality of your spiritual life will have a direct impact on the quality of your family life. Prayer changes things and people, including your children. So pray constantly for your youngsters. God is listening, and He wants to hear from you ... Now.

Speaking
mom-ese

Write down the names of your children and some of the concerns and goals you have for each one of them. Then pray specifically about those issues.

_____

_____

_____
_____
_____
_____
_____
_____
_____
_____
_____
_____
_____
_____
_____
_____

Prayer

Lord, thank You for the gift of prayer. I would feel hopeless if I thought raising these children was completely up to me. Thank You for not only parenting from the inside out, but also for equipping me to parent from the outside in. I'm so glad we're partners in this business of parenting.

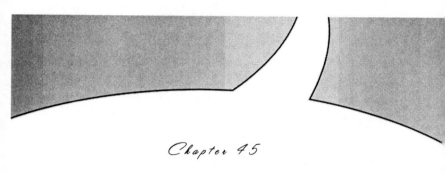

Chapter 45

meeting beth moore

. . . .

**Now all of you together are Christ's body, and each
one of you is a separate and necessary part of it.**

1 Corinthians 12:27 NLT

The first time I met author and speaker Beth Moore, I was ecstatic. In fact, Steve and the kids got sick of hearing me talk about it. To me, meeting Beth was more exciting than going to the presidential inauguration, shooting hoops with George Clooney, singing at the Emmys, or having Tom Cruise show up in *The Facts of Life* rehearsal hall.

Let's pause for a little bit of "girl talk," because I know you want the details! She wore an adorable, hot pink sweater. Her hair was pulled back, and it showed off her big, bright eyes and beautiful laughing smile. She looked younger, prettier, and even tinier than she does on her videos. (If I didn't love her so much I would hate her.)

We enjoyed a delightful conversation, a delicious meal, and split a piece of sugar-free cheesecake. We talked mostly about our families, a little about ministry, and a wee bit about business. As we talked, I had several "out of body" experiences, thinking, *I'm sitting across the table from Beth Moore!*

It was an absolutely fabulous evening, but I must confess that over the next couple of days, I struggled with wishing I could be more like Beth Moore. As I walked around the ballroom praying for the MomTime Get-A-Way I was hosting that weekend, I told God, *I want to be that deep into Bible study. Better yet, I want to be that deep, period.* Next to the obvious intensity of her relationship with God, I felt downright shallow.

Throughout the retreat, though, God gently chastised me by reminding me that we are all unique parts of the body of Christ (see 1 Corinthians 12:26–28). That weekend, the Lord refreshed the moms through laughter, chocolate, gifts, massages, cozy sheets, and a good night's sleep. He wrapped His Abba arms around them and reassured His girls that He saw how hard they were working, the sacrifices they were making, the sleep they were losing, and the little lives they were changing.

I understood then that these moms would leave the Get-A-Way having been touched by God in a different way than if they had attended a Beth Moore Living Proof conference. I also realized that sometimes we need a stronger, more intense touch from God—like iron sharpening iron—and sometimes we need a softer touch from Him—the kind that gently strokes our weary cheek and wipes away our tears.

Friend, I hope you never wish to be me, because then we would lose you, and the world doesn't need another Lisa Whelchel or even another Beth Moore. God created you for a specific job at a specific time that nobody else can fill. I can't love on your neighbor, forgive your husband, or adore your children. God has put these people—and many others—in your life for *you* to touch. Your touch may ultimately reach millions or it may impact just one person that no one could reach but you.

You know something? I can't wait to meet you. It thrills me to think that someday we'll be able to sit down to share a piece of cheesecake in heaven (it surely won't be sugar free!), and I will have made a new friend just as special as Beth Moore.

· ◀

Speaking
mom-ese

Make a list of the people you admire
and the things you appreciate about
them. Now make a list of traits you
admire in yourself. Come on—you
can do it! _____

_____

_____
_____
_____
_____
_____
_____
_____
_____
_____
_____
_____
_____
_____
_____
_____
_____
_____
_____
_____

Prayer
Lord, thank You for putting mentors and giants of the faith in my path.
As I look up to them, may my eyes focus on worshipping only You.
Remind me to view myself in light of the Creator and not the creation.

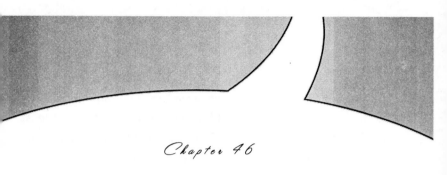

making lemonade
out of lemons

. . . .

**The mind of man plans his way,
but the LORD directs his steps.**

Proverbs 16:9 NASB

$\mathcal{S}$teve loves the band Avalon. I heard they were coming to the Dallas area, so I bought tickets, marked Steve's calendar, arranged for a babysitter, and told him I was taking him out on a surprise date. I then bought Avalon's newest CD and made reservations at Steve's favorite restaurant. My plan was to have the waiter present Steve the CD along with the bill. I stuck a note on the disc that read, "Wouldn't it be fun to hear these songs live and in person?"

Well, nothing went as planned. First, there was a terrible accident on the freeway, so it took us two hours to get to the restaurant.

By the time we arrived, it was too late to eat and still make it to the concert, so I had to tell Steve about the surprise. At least I thought it was a surprise. Steve confessed that he had gone to Avalon's web site and discovered they were coming to town. When he checked the date on the calendar, he saw that it was the same day as our surprise date. He put two and two together and played along with the charade.

I was disappointed, but we made the most of it by eating at our favorite fast food restaurant before heading to the church venue. Once there, our romantic date took another hard knock. I had reserved seats up front and arranged for us to meet the band after the concert. When we arrived, though, I discovered that my e-mails hadn't been passed all the way down the chain of command, so we ended up sitting about eight rows from the back of the huge sanctuary.

Since the concert started at seven o'clock, I had told the babysitter we would be home by ten. But I didn't figure on there being two opening acts. Avalon didn't even go onstage until nine! We were only able to hear a few of their songs before we had to get back home. Fortunately, by that time we were ready. After two hours of listening to very loud music and standing up the whole time, Steve and I decided that we were getting too old for that kind of party life anyway.

There is an old Jewish proverb that says, "If you want to give God a good laugh, tell Him your plans!" How true. Every day life is filled with surprises—some good and some not so good. But even when our plans get derailed, God remains faithful. He always finds ways to make lemonade out of our lemons.

The story of Steve's and my disaster date is silly, but the truth behind it is real: if we're serious about surrendering our lives to God, then we probably shouldn't get too upset when He does things a bit differently than we would have liked. It is good and right to make plans, but it is even more godly and righteous to allow God to change them.

. . . .

Speaking
mom-ese

Write down some of the plans you have
made recently. Now make a point to
surrender them to God. Refer to
them later and see how many of
your plans God changed because
He had a better idea. _____

_____

_____

_____

_____

_____

_____

_____

_____

_____

_____

_____

_____

_____

_____

_____

_____

_____

_____

Prayer

Dear Lord, I want to be a diligent servant and make wise plans, but I also
want to be flexible enough to allow You to change them however You see fit.
Teach me how to find and maintain this balance.

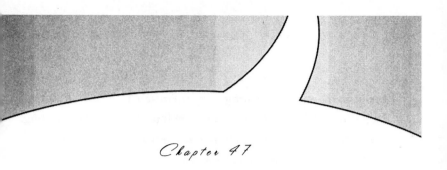

catch that thief

. . . .

**Submit therefore to God. Resist the devil
and he will flee from you.**

James 4:7 NASB

*O*ur neighborhood was having a Christmas lights contest, and Steve had signed up to be one of the judges. I was excited about the opportunity to create a wonderful family memory. In my mind, the whole family would pile into the minivan; I would pop in my favorite Christmas CD, *Christmas Sing-Along with Mitch*, a childhood staple; we would head to Jack in the Box for a chicken sandwich, a family tradition; and then we would drive through the neighborhood enjoying and rating the lights. Later, I would make a scrapbook page of it all.

We made it as far as piling in the minivan and popping in the CD. On the way to Jack in the Box, all hell broke loose (I mean that), and the evening went up in smoke. The kids started bickering with each other. I started yelling at them to stop yelling. Steve clammed up and wouldn't say a word. And I pouted and said, "Take me home. I don't want to play anymore!"

I stomped into the house, threw myself on the bed, and didn't come out for the rest of the night. Haven went to her room crying, Tucker went to his room yelling, and Clancy wisely stayed out of the line of fire. It was the last night of the competition, so Steve had to go ahead and judge the houses. I was so disappointed. The devil had crept in and stolen from our family, and we had just let him! We all repented, kissed, and made up the next morning, but by that time Satan had already won the battle.

The next day, I berated myself, thinking, *When will I learn that every time I lose self-control, we all end up losing? I should have stopped in the middle of the chaos and insisted that we pray. I should have seen with spiritual eyes that we were dealing with the enemy, who comes to steal, kill, and destroy.*

We don't have to stand by and watch Satan destroy our families. The Lord tells us exactly what to do in such circumstances: we're to resist the devil and rebuke the father of lies. Jesus was the best at this. Each time He came face-to-face with the enemy, He responded with, "It is written," and fought Satan with words straight from the holy Scriptures. So the next time you wake up and realize that the argument you're having really isn't about your husband or your kids but instead about the devil trying to divide your family, stand firm and remember Jesus' promise to you: "Behold, I give you the authority to trample on serpents and scorpions, and over all the power of the enemy, and nothing shall by any means hurt you" (Luke 10:19 NKJV).

· ·

Speaking
mom-ese

What turmoil or conflict are you facing? Ask God to help you see with spiritual eyes what is truly happening. Then take the authority Jesus gives you, and write a prayer that draws a line in the sand (with the blood of Jesus). Make it known to the enemy that because of the cross, he is not allowed to step over that line. _____

_____
_____
_____
_____
_____
_____
_____
_____
_____
_____

Prayer

In Jesus' name, I take authority over the power of the enemy. I will no longer stand by and watch the devil kill, steal, and destroy my family or hurt us in any way. Thank You, Lord, for Your words of encouragement, which tell me, "You, dear children, are from God and have overcome them, because the one who is in you is greater than the one who is in the world" (1 John 4:4 NIV).

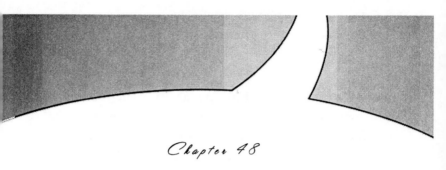

Chapter 48

itchy ears

. . . .

**For the time will come when men will not put up
with sound doctrine. Instead, to suit their own desires, they will gather around them a great number
of teachers to say what their itching ears want to
hear. They will turn their ears away from the truth
and turn aside to myths.**

2 Timothy 4:3–4 NIV

$\mathcal{I}$was at a meeting when a prayer request was made for a
deaf baby scheduled to receive a cochlear implant. The baby's
parents asked for prayers that the surgery would go well so
the baby would be able to hear and speak. They also requested
prayer that the baby's recovery would not be too traumatic—the
doctors had warned them that their child, upon hearing sounds
for the first time, would probably scream and cry for days.

Immediately, I was struck by the similarities between that
little baby and the rest of us. Sometimes, even as grownups, we
would rather not listen to things that we should be anxious to

hear. Why? Because our instincts take over and tell us to block out anything new or foreign. Think about the irony of this baby's situation. Her mother's sweet voice, her brother's laughter, even the sound of her daddy singing a lullaby will initially make this baby cry and cover her ears. And yet, how many of us react the same way when we hear the words *sin, obedience,* or *sacrifice*? Far too many! Our heavenly Father knows that these are words of love that will bring redemption, blessings, and meaning to our lives, but like that tiny baby, we would rather block out His voice and retreat to our world of the comfortable and familiar.

God offers each of us the priceless gift of eternal life, but in order to receive that blessing, we must first acknowledge that we are sinners. God wants to guide us, but all too often we refuse to listen and obey. It must break God's heart when we choose our own way rather than the abundant life He offers! Like our heavenly Father does, the baby's parents love her so much that they are willing to do what they feel is best for her—at great cost. They know the transition will be difficult, that their little girl will fight the gift she is being given, but they are willing to sacrifice everything to do what they believe is best for her in the long run.

Do you know someone who is desperately fighting to avoid the words of God? Are you ignoring a family member you know you should confront—possibly at great cost to yourself—to warn him or her about heading in the wrong direction? Are you brave enough to shed light on a friend's misbehavior and call it sin? If so, don't be surprised if the response you receive is similar to that of the baby's: tears, screaming, and covered ears. But if the other person is willing to hear the truth, then in time your words may become as familiar and comfortable as a mother's voice, a brother's laughter, or a father's lullaby.

• •

Speaking
mom-ese

Think of someone you know whose ears are closed to words of life because hearing the truth would be too painful or cost too much. Do you love that person enough to speak up, even if your words will be unwelcome? Determine what actions you should take and then ask God for the strength to follow through. _____

_____

_____

_____

_____

_____

_____

_____

_____

_____

_____

_____

_____

_____

_____

_____

Prayer

*Lord, I give You permission to perform surgery on the ears of my heart.
If I have refused to hear You, or my ears are full of the "wax" of my own way,
or I am simply turning from Your higher purpose, then please work
a miracle and allow me to hear Your voice. Hold me close if I cry or scream,
but do not let me go until I have received the sweet sounds of Your Spirit
whispering in my ear.*

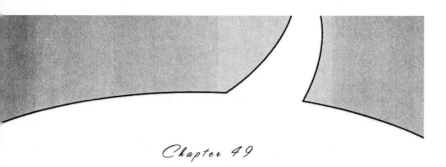

Chapter 49

the gardener knows best

. . . .

"I am the true vine, and My Father is the vine-
dresser. Every branch in Me that does not bear
fruit, He takes away; and every branch that bears
fruit, He prunes it so that it may bear more fruit."

John 15:1–2 NASB

You know how it is. When God is working on a certain area of your life, it seems like everywhere you turn He is repeating something He's already told you a hundred times. (It sounds like how I parent my own kids!)

By letting His voice echo in my heart and mind, the Lord has taught me a bunch of great lessons. For example, He constantly reminds me that the way the world measures success— even the way I measure success—is not necessarily the way He defines it. He also has to tell me again and again that I need to focus on saying no and making sure I'm prioritizing my time well, putting the rocks into my Mason jar before I pour in the sand.

Often, His lessons surprise me. One particular time, I distinctively felt Him telling me not to wake up so early to spend time with Him. I love nothing better than to get up before dawn and to have a long, leisurely morning alone with Jesus. But in doing so, I was getting wiped out by dinnertime and ready to fall into bed by nine o'clock. Jesus caught me off guard when He pointed out that my "window times" with the kids—our special time for those heart-to-heart chats—were getting shorter and shorter when I put them to bed at night. Meanwhile, the kids needed to talk to me more than ever. The Lord nudged me gently, saying, *Lisa, you need to get up later and spend a bit less structured time with Me so you can stay awake and hear what is on your kids' hearts when they are ready and willing to talk. We'll have plenty of time to talk throughout the day and even more time when they are grown.*

Another area God has worked in my life—in fact, on our whole family—has been in honoring the Sabbath. Resting is a challenge for me. I actually enjoy working; it makes me feel good to be productive. But God knew what He was talking about when He commanded us to work six days and rest one. He has taught me that keeping the Sabbath is all about trust: do I believe that by obeying God, I will get everything accomplished that He desires?

This concept has been even more difficult for Steve, who is a bigger workaholic than I am! But God works in mysterious ways. One Sunday, Steve found a Post-it note on his computer screen that read, "Don't turn on the computer on Sundays. — God." The handwriting was suspiciously adolescent, but I guess that if God wrote the note with His fingertip, His writing could be a bit scribbly.

It took a few months, but once Steve, urged on by God's little helpers, joined the rest of us in honoring the Sabbath, each Sunday became a new adventure. Now the whole family looks forward to Sundays, and we've started a bunch of great traditions. After church, we try out a new restaurant somewhere in the Dallas/Fort Worth metroplex. Then it's naptime. When everyone wakes up, I sneak in a few hours scrapbooking, Steve chills out in front of the TV, and the kids hang out in their rooms. Finally, we rent a DVD and have a family movie night, complete with snuggling and pizza.

The lessons the Lord has taught me are precious. In fact, I'm learning to love His pruning shears. I don't always understand why He cuts away certain branches, but I do know that by staying connected to Him, I will bear fruit that lasts.

. . . .

Speaking
mom-ese

Do you struggle to obey God because
His instructions don't make sense to
you? What areas of your life are you
resisting His pruning? Write a quick
note to the Gardener and ask Him
to trim as much as He wants.

_____

_____

_____

_____

_____

_____

_____

_____

_____

_____

_____

_____

_____

_____

_____

_____

_____

_____

_____

Prayer
Lord, I will trust You even when I don't understand Your ways.
Pruning is one of those areas. It hurts, and sometimes You cut away good
things in my life that I'm not ready to give up. Help me to relax and
submit to Your expert shaping.

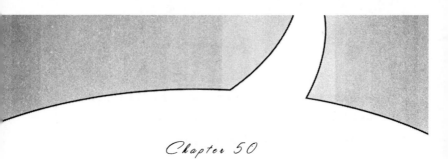

Chapter 50

God will take care of everything—the rest is up to you

. . . .

For anyone who enters God's rest also rests from his own work, just as God did from his.

Hebrews 4:10 NIV

*D*uring one of my morning quiet times, I was reading in Hebrews chapters 3 and 4, which talk about entering into God's rest. I'd just experienced a night of unrest, so my interest was especially piqued. My anxiety was nothing serious, just the normal things: Worried about my children and some of the attitudes I'd seen sneaking out of their hearts. Overwhelmed at the task before me of writing the *Creative Correction* Bible study. Concerned about spending money on a new washer and dryer at the same time we were finally getting window treatments up in the house. Distressed over the busyness of our lives and wondering how to change that. Anxious about my cousin, Christal, who had a mysterious infection.

These weren't Third World-sized problems, but they were huge in my little universe, and I just didn't know how I would be able to give up worrying about them. At least if I could come up with a handful of solutions on my own, I reasoned, I would feel some measure of control.

I told the Lord that I trusted Him—but I knew that if I *really* believed He was in control, I would be able to lay my concerns at His feet and then rest easy. The Bible said it was possible. The Apostle Paul said God had promised it! So how could I actually do it?

God began to guide me. As I reread the chapters in Hebrews, I started to put together my own little recipe for rest. Following this method of prayer has helped me, and I hope it can be an encouragement to you, too.

Remember God's character.

They always go astray in their heart, and they did not know My ways. —Hebrews 3:10b NASB

Begin by praising God for His character, including His goodness, love, mercy, and power. Remember that He can and wants to answer your prayers.

Recount His faithfulness.

As in the day of trial in the wilderness, where your fathers tried Me by testing Me, and saw My works for forty years.
—Hebrews 3:8b–9 NASB

Recount times when the Lord answered your prayers and proved His character to you.

Recite this reminder.

Jesus Christ is the same yesterday, today, and forever.
—Hebrews 13:8 NKJV

Knowing God's character and remembering His faithfulness to you in the past will give you confidence that He will not forsake you now.

Reexamine your motives.

Nothing in all creation can hide from him. Everything is naked and exposed before his eyes. —Hebrews 4:13a NLT

Ask yourself, does this prayer request line up with God's will and character? Will the resolution bring Him glory?

Recruit a prayer partner.

But encourage one another daily, as long as it is called Today, so that none of you may be hardened by sin's deceitfulness. —*Hebrews 3:13* NIV

If possible, share your request with someone else. There is power in unity, and a good friend who will speak the truth will bring you encouragement.

Receive His promises.

For the word of God is living and active and sharper than any two-edged sword, and piercing as far as the division of soul and spirit, of both joints and marrow, and able to judge the thoughts and intentions of the heart. —*Hebrews 4:12* NASB

Find a Scripture upon which you can base your confidence and faith that He will hear your prayers.

Request your heart's desires.

Be anxious for nothing, but in everything by prayer and supplication with thanksgiving let your requests be made known to God. And the peace of God, which surpasses all comprehension, will guard your hearts and your minds in Christ Jesus. —*Philippians 4:6–7* NASB

Tell God what is on your heart.

Resolve to believe.

Therefore let us be diligent to enter that rest. —Hebrews 4:11 NASB

Choose to believe—faith is an act of the will.

Respect God's authority and submit to His will.

For every house is built by someone, but the builder of all things is God. —Hebrews 3:4 NASB

Surrender the outcome to His higher wisdom.

Release it to God.

For anyone who enters God's rest also rests from his own work, just as God did from his.—Hebrews 4:10 NIV

Let it go and don't pick it up again.

Rest in Him!

For we who have believed enter that rest. —Hebrews 4:3a NASB

Don't worry about it—your heart's desire is in good hands.

· ·

Speaking mom-ese

What are you worried about? Make a list of things and then systematically pray through the "Recipe for Rest" for each anxiety. _____

_____

_____

_____
_____
_____
_____
_____
_____
_____
_____
_____
_____
_____
_____
_____
_____
_____
_____
_____
_____
_____
_____
_____
_____

Prayer

*Dear Lord, I choose to enter Your rest. As I bring You each of my concerns,
I will thank You in advance, knowing that You hear me and will answer
according to Your will and in Your own way. Now I ask for Your peace to
guard my heart and mind.*

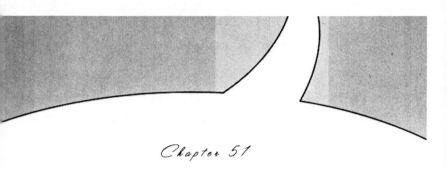

created for good works

· ·

**For we are God's workmanship, created in Christ
Jesus to do good works, which God prepared in
advance for us to do.**

Ephesians 2:10 NIV

I was having dinner with a friend when she asked if I found
it challenging to travel with my husband. Now, I always try to
travel with Steve and often with the kids, too. I've never done it
any other way. But I thought about her question the next time I
was scheduled to speak.

I had about an hour and a half before I was to go on stage,
and I was attempting to prepare both my heart and my face—
both of which needed my undivided attention. First, Clancy
walked into the room and asked to borrow my hairbrush. The
next thing I knew, she was standing in front of the mirror, singing into the "microphone." I smiled and tried to remind myself

that it was important to be thankful that the teenage hormones hadn't kicked in yet and made her too embarrassed to rock out in front of her mom.

Then the phone rang. "Hon," Steve said from the other line, "will you order some room service for me? When it's there, call me and I'll come up and have dinner with you." Steve was working, too, setting up the room where I was speaking, but I wanted to tell him, "Order it yourself!" Instead, I dutifully picked up the phone and ordered a club sandwich and a diet cola and reminded myself to be thankful that cooking could be as easy as picking up the telephone.

I had just gotten back to praying about the upcoming conference when my cell phone rang. For the next fifteen minutes I bounced between feelings of frustration (over so many interruptions), guilt (over feeling frustrated), and fear (because I only had a little bit of time left to prepare myself).

As I fretted about not having time to prepare, a Scripture popped into my head: "For we are God's workmanship, created in Christ Jesus to do good works, which God prepared in advance for us to do" (Ephesians 2:10 NIV). In an instant I realized what God was saying to me. I didn't feel prepared, but He was. Any good works that He had planned for me to do would most certainly be taken care of by Him. So I changed course. As I waited for Steve to come upstairs, I dressed and finished my makeup. Then I took a few minutes to pray. *Lord, work in me, through*

Christ Jesus, the good things You have prepared for me to do, I requested silently. My "work" is to walk in faith, believing that You can do through me—or even in spite of me—anything that You desire, whether or not I feel prepared.

I heard Steve's knock at the door, and I was ready—ready to sit down and enjoy sharing a sandwich, a diet cola, and the company of a man who, after so many years, still wants to eat every meal sitting across the table from me.

Speaking mom-ese

Write down a few of the good works you believe God wants you to accomplish. Then express your confidence that God can and will help you finish what He intends for you to do.

_____
_____
_____
_____
_____
_____
_____
_____
_____

Prayer
Lord, I want to accomplish what You have planned for me—no more and no less. I submit my days, minutes, and plans to You and ask for You to achieve Your purpose in me however You see fit. Help me to trust in You and not in my own abilities.

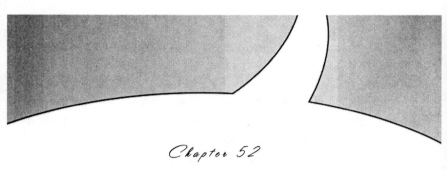

Chapter 52

Jesus loves the
little children

. . . .

**How great is the love the Father has lavished on us,
that we should be called children of God!
And that is what we are!**

1 John 3:1 NIV

I was speaking at a church in Nashville. Before I stepped to the platform, the children's choir performed. As I watched them sing their little hearts out, I saw their parents and grandparents beam with pride. *I bet that's how God feels when He watches us, His little children,* I thought, smiling.

Then I began to notice all the different personalities represented on the stage. A little girl in the front row was showing—well, *pushing*—all the other little girls to the spot where they were supposed to be standing. A few tykes over, a small boy was crying and scanning the crowd for his mother so he could run off the stage and be held safely in her arms. My favorite, though, was the little boy who thought he was the only child worth watching. He was bowing and mugging and making funny faces, trying through sheer magnetism to attract all the attention. Thankfully, he was so distracting that few people noticed the boy behind him who was dying a thousand deaths because he didn't know the words to the songs and clearly felt stupid in his new suit.

Each of these children was adorable. I doubt even one person in the audience watched the "bossy" little girl and thought, *She's too controlling and domineering. She needs to stop trying to fix everybody else and look at her own sins*. I can't imagine that anyone considered the teary boy a worthless wimp because he wanted to run off and find his mother. I could see that everyone was laughing at the little show-off rather than judging him as a conceited egomaniac. And I think each person in the crowd could relate to the boy who looked lost and uncomfortable, not knowing what to do.

The next time you wonder how God feels about you, consider how you feel when you watch little children act like little children. Or, if you find it difficult to think of God as a parent because your own parents were not good examples, imagine God as your grandfather. There were an awful lot of grandparents in the audience, and they had the broadest smiles of all.

I find it amazing that God chose to compare His love with

that of a parent—the same love that cleans up vomit, wipes bottoms, and stays up all night with children who have little to offer except highly contagious germs. But you know what? God is happy to do it, because that's what loving parents do.

• •

Speaking mom-ese

Write down some of the quirks or unique characteristics you see in yourself and in your children. Now write down the way you think that God, as your heavenly Father, views these qualities. _____

_____

_____

_____

_____

_____

_____

_____

_____

_____

_____

_____

_____

_____

Prayer

Father, thank You for loving me like a parent would. Remind me to cut myself and others some slack when I am tempted to judge. Help me to find the balance between acting like a child and coming to You as a child.

LaVergne, TN USA
17 March 2011
220535LV00010B/2/P